The Extraordinary Projects Bible

The Extraordinary Projects Bible

Duct Tape Tote Bags, Homemade Rockets, and Other Awesome Projects Anyone Can Make

Instructables.com

Skyhorse Publishing

Skyhorse Publishing books may be purchased in bulk at special discounts for sales promotion, corporate gifts, fund-raising, or educational purposes. Special editions can also be created to specifications. For details, contact the Special Sales Department, Skyhorse Publishing, 307 West 36th Street, 11th Floor, New York, NY 10018 or info@ skyhorsepublishing.com.

Skyhorse® and Skyhorse Publishing® are registered trademarks of Skyhorse Publishing, Inc.®, a Delaware corporation.

Visit our website at www.skyhorsepublishing.com.

10 9 8 7 6 5 4 3 2 1

Library of Congress Cataloging-in-Publication Data is available on file.

This 2014 edition printed for Barnes & Noble, Inc.
ISBN: 978-1-62636-430-1

Printed in China

Disclaimer:

This book is intended to offer general guidance. It is sold with the understanding that every effort was made to provide the most current and accurate information. However, errors and omissions are still possible. Any use or misuse of the information contained herein is solely the responsibility of the user, and the author and publisher make no warrantees or claims as to the truth or validity of the information. The author and publisher shall have neither liability nor responsibility to any person or entity with respect to any loss or damage caused, or alleged to have been caused, directly or indirectly, by the information contained in this book. Furthermore, this book is not intended to give professional dietary, technical, or medical advice. Please refer to and follow any local laws when using any of the information contained herein, and act responsibly and safely at all times.

Table of Contents

table of contents

Introduction

Like a do-it-yourself rocket, *The Bible of Extraordinary Projects* will carry you to new heights of creativity and imagination. Using readily available materials, you'll make useful or fanciful items that are sure to impress and delight.

"Awesome Projects from Unexpected Places" contains fifteen projects that repurpose everyday items to create unique home furnishings and gifts for friends and relatives and to inspire you to come up with ideas of your own.

"Practical Duct Tape Projects" has seven opportunities to make any or all of a mind-boggling array of items made solely from duct tape, that ubiquitous item found in every toolbox and utility drawer.

"Backyard Rockets" includes eleven both simple and more complicated projects that appeal to everyone who ever dreamed of constructing and launching projectiles to reach the stars . . . or just the other side of your backyard.

"Projects to Get You Off the Grid" showcases twelve ways to achieve self-sufficiency and environmental awareness through the use of solar and wind power, rainwater collection, and poultry raising.

Each project comes with clear step-by-step instructions and, where appropriate, advice about using the item. In addition, each project has a reference to a website URL where components, construction, and advice offer complementary instructions and illustrations.

Instructables.com is the most popular project-sharing community on the Internet, and part of the Autodesk family of creative communities. Since August 2005, Instructables has provided easy publishing tools to enable passionate, creative people to share their most innovative projects, recipes, skills, and ideas. Instructables has over one hundred thousand projects covering all subjects, including crafts, art, electronics, kids, home improvements, pets, outdoors, reuse, bikes, cars, robotics, food, decorating, woodworking, costuming, games, and more.

Awesome Projects

I found half a wine barrel that the local pub was throwing out, so I grabbed it because it was made out of oak, and I would hate to see that in someone's fireplace.

Step 1: The Barrel

The half-barrel that I found was almost ready to fall to pieces. Two of the bands had fallen off and the top one was also ready to fall off. It would be very difficult to reassemble, so I carefully put the bands back on and took it home.

I was not sure what to make until I saw the nice graphics on the top, so I sanded the top back and put furniture oil on it. It looked good, so I decided to keep the graphic, which would mean keeping the top intact. My first thought was a coffee table. But as the project

progressed, the misses said she liked the height of the table and would like it on the deck next to her chair.

Step 2: Stuff You Will Need
- Sandpaper grits 40, 80, 120, 240
- Matt black paint
- 3 or 4 coach bolts with washers and nuts
- Drill and dill bits
- 3 or 4 wood screws
- Small nail or tacks
- Hammer
- Jig saw (reciprocating saw)
- Clean rags
- Your favorite timber finish
- Angle grinder, with sanding disc
- About 2 hours
- Beer

Step 3: Mark Out the Legs

I decided to make the table with three legs, as they don't rock around on uneven surfaces, so I marked out the three slats that were going to be used for legs. I then made sure the bands were straight and tight and then drilled and screwed the three slates to the bottom band so nothing would move in the next steps.

Step 4: Remove the Sharp Bits

The top band had quite a sharp edge on it, so I used a grinder with a sanding disc to remove the edge and make it smooth.

Step 5: Remove the Bands and Paint

I removed the top two bands with a hammer and a block of wood and then cleaned them with thinners. I hung them from the roof with wire and spray painted matt black. I also painted the heads of the coach bolts.

Step 6: Sanding

I used four different grit sandpapers starting with 40, then 80, 120, and 240. I only sanded the top and the top of the sides and the legs. Sanding is boring so I got some free child labor to do most of it.

Step 8: Refit the Top Band

I put the top band back on and knocked it down with a hammer.

Step 7: Oiling

You could probably do this step last, but I put a coat of my favorite furniture oil on early so it would be under the bands, helping protect the timber from spills and moisture. Just use a rag to rub the oil on.

Step 9: Cut Out the Legs

Next, I drilled three holes big enough for my jig saw blade to pass through and cut around the bottom of the line that the second band had left. I found that oak was very hard and difficult to cut with a dull blade. I should really have put a new blade in the saw, but the store was closed. Don't forget to leave the legs uncut. The waste wood can then be removed.

Step 10: Fitting the Second Band

The second band can now be fitted. I knocked it down with a hammer and a block of wood and drilled three holes through the band and the legs, into which the coach bolts were fitted. To help keep the top band in place, I drilled three small holes and nailed in some carpet tacks that had an old style black head, which matched the look of the table.

Step 11: Remove the Bottom Band

Now that the table has been bolted together, the bottom band can be removed and the legs sanded and finished off. The misses likes the height of the table, but it could be cut down for a coffee table.

Step 12: Other stuff

I think, now that it's finished, it would look better with four legs, and it needs to be a bit shorter, as the curve on the end of the legs make it look a bit odd. But it is very stable, doesn't rock around, and the ring around the top stops my drunk friends from putting their glasses on the edge of the table, which always inevitably leads to their beers getting knocked over.

Concrete Lamp

By Ethan Lacy (hands_on)
(http://www.instructables.com/
id/concrete-lamp/)

This is a lamp made of concrete, glass, and steel.

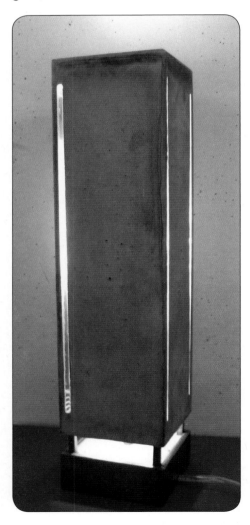

Step 1: Stuff You'll Need

- Concrete (Rockite works best) and something to mix it in/with
- Something to make formwork (Plywood or melamine work well. Foam Core can also be used.)
- 16" of 1.5" × ¼" steel bar stock
- 3 pieces of glass: ¼" thick: 12" × 4"; ⅛" thick: 12" × 3.5"; 1/16" thick: 12" × 3.5" (You can cut these yourself, or, easier yet, have a glass store cut them. They need to be fairly precise.)
- Screws, drill, drill bits, driver
- Foam core
- Glue gun
- Ceramic lamp socket
- 4" threaded lamp post
- Light bulb (bright)
- Lamp cord
- Lamp switch
- Screwdriver
- Space to make a mess
- Free time

Step 2: Making the Outer Formwork

First, you need to make the formwork. This will make or break (literally) this project. The more precise you can make it, the better. The inside volume needs to be exactly 4" square. You can use melamine, which will give a smooth surface. You can also use lumber or plywood, which can give the concrete texture. If you use ¾" material, you'll need two pieces 4" × 14", two at 5.5" × 14", and one for the bottom (which is actually the top) at 5.5" square. Again, make this as precise as possible. If you don't have access to a shop, you can use ½" foam core, a knife, and a ruler. Use a glue gun to glue it all together. If you coat the inside surface of the foam core with clear packing tape, the concrete won't stick, and you'll get a smooth, glassy surface on the concrete. The foam core method is probably easier and less forgiving, and works pretty much in the same way. Just make sure to seal the joints really well with the glue gun or packing tape. Otherwise, it will leak. Everywhere. The concrete will be very liquid-y. Like heavy cream. Don't underestimate its ability to find cracks and leak out of them.

Step 3: Make the Lamp Base

You can do this many different ways. I used steel filled with Rockite (concrete). This requires welding and grinding equipment. You can also just cast a hunk of concrete. Or, a block of wood. Just remember that you need to get the cord in there somehow. I used ¼" thick steel bar stock at 1.5" wide. To make a 4" square, you need two at 4" and two at 3.5". Weld these together and grind the welds. Then, because I'm going to pour concrete into the volume, I welded two little pieces of

¼" bar to keep the hunk of concrete from slipping out someday. Then drill a ¼" hole as far to the bottom as possible on one of the sides. This is for the cord.

We won't fill the bottom all the way with concrete, so that the cord can come out of the post and out our little hole. So put in a piece of foam core to the top level of the hole we just drilled. Seal the edges with the glue gun. We'll pour the concrete from the top. Then, with the glue gun, glue the threaded rod post onto the foam core. Make sure it's not off at an angle. The last two photos are what it looks like when it's dry, top and bottom. Get the idea? I think the next time I do this, I'll probably forget about floating it above the base. I think a hunk of wood could look nice. This took too long.

Now for our first pour. This will be good practice for the big one. I recommend getting Rockite. It's available at a lot of smaller hardware stores. The stuff is awesome. It's like plaster, just a lot stronger, and it has a beautiful smooth finish. Mix it as per the instructions so that it's like heavy cream. Or melted ice cream. Not too runny! The more water, the weaker. It's easy to add too much water. Add it slowly.

Pour it in just short of the top of the steel base. Now, this is the annoying part. I don't think I would do this again this way, but here goes. I wanted the thing to "float" off the base a bit. So I decided to cast in some ¼" steel bar legs. I welded these little bits of wire on to the legs so that it would adhere well to the concrete. I won't get into the details, because I think it's a bit of a cockamamied way to do this. But you need to make sure the wire won't interfere with the glass for the main pour.

For this step, I'm just setting them into the base about ¼", so that the shade will sit securely into the base. These will be easy to remove once it's hard, and then I'll cast the legs into the shade. I know, ridiculous. The trick is you have to somehow hold these little guys in position while the concrete dries. This can be accomplished with small clamps. Or maybe duct tape. But have a game plan before you pour. I didn't have one, so this is my improvised, half-assed on-the-spot effort. It worked, mainly because Rockite dries fast. It will start to set up in about fifteen minutes. After an hour, you can carve it with a blade. In twenty-four hours, it's wicked hard, but you can sand it and shape it a bit. After a week it's rock solid.

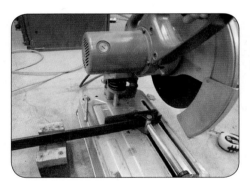

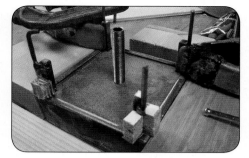

Step 4: Preparing the Mold

You'll need to build some formwork for the void in the middle. I used foam core and melamine. I think it would be better to use all foam core, or a solid piece of rigid insulation foam (usually pink or blue, available at Home Depot). The reason for this is because you have to get it out once the concrete dries. I thought the foam core would be squishable enough. But it was a pain to get it out. So, use foam, and you can coat it in packing tape for a better finish and easier release. Regardless, it needs to be 3" square, exactly, and the same length as the outer mold, *plus* the amount you want it to "float" above the base, if you want to do that. I used ¾". This way, the base can rest on this while we cast the feet into the shade, and it'll keep the right spacing (see photos).

You can glue the glass directly to the inner formwork, as shown. This way, the glass will be exposed on the inside of the shade. This glue will come off easily when you release it. The thick piece of glass overhangs ½" on either side of the inner formwork. The other two pieces butt into it and overhang ½" on their respective sides. Obviously, you can modify this layout. There should be at least ¾" on the top and bottom. This is critical so that the concrete has some structure, since we're cutting it all up with the glass. Now slide it into the outer formwork. This might require loosening some screws. This is not an easy step. You'll have to futz with it. If your measurements were good, it will be easier.

It's critical that the glass butts into the outer formwork, exposing the edge and ensuring that it is securely glued to the inner formwork, as well as exposing the inside so the light can get out. This will take patience. Trial, error, adjust. The last step: Once the formwork is adjusted, tight, and sealed (you can use the glue gun like caulk if need be), invert the base over the top so that you can cast the legs into the shade. Make sure they're reasonably straight and that everything looks good. Take it out.

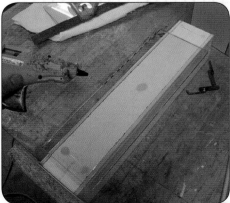

Step 5: The Big Pour

Mix up enough Rockite. I'll leave this up to you to figure out. Pour it slowly into the mold, until it comes flush with the top edge. You can overfill it a bit and then scrape it flush after about ten minutes. Invert the base over it to cast in the legs. You can glue these temporarily into the base with a glue gun or use duct tape or something. You don't want to lose them to the concrete abyss. Once it all looks good, put it away for at least twelve hours.

Step 6: Break the Mold

Take off the base, but leave the sides attached. It's tempting to look, but it'll be easier and safer to ream out the middle if you leave the sides attached. If you used solid foam, get a big, fat, long drill bit and ream it out as much as possible. Stick screwdrivers in there, putty knives, whatever you need to do to get that foam out. Foam core is the same deal. Needle-nose pliers and yanking might help. This step is a pain in the ass. Take your time and be gentle. It's possible to break this thing.

After you get the center pretty well cleaned out, you can take the outer mold off. Make sure it didn't crack anywhere. (If it did, you can fix cracks with superglue.) You might need to excavate the glass edges a bit so they are exposed. Be gentle. You can use a flat edge screwdriver to do this. You might also need to do this on the inside if some of the Rockite got in between the formwork and the glass. It should chip off. Be gentle. Finally, you can lightly sand the sharp corners and rinse the whole thing off in the sink. Make sure all the glass is exposed cleanly inside and out. If it came out on the first try, nice work. If not, hopefully you can reuse the glass and repour.

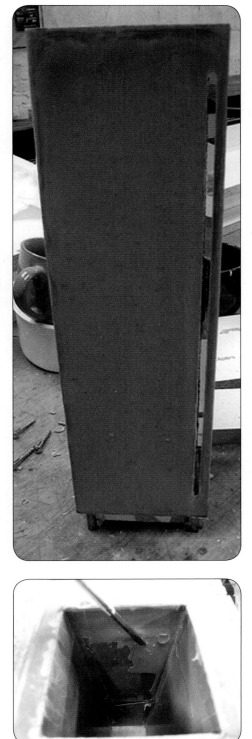

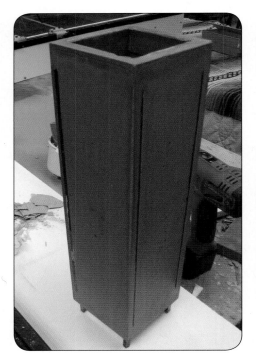

Step 7: Assemble Lamp

Put the lamp together. Thread the cord up through the base holes and screw the thing on top. You can put a switch on the cord too, if you want. I'm not getting into wiring here. If you don't know what you're doing, ask someone who does.

Use a bright bulb. I used fluorescent (incandescents will get the thing really hot—better to use compact fluorescents and less energy at the same time). This bulb is a 150 watt equivalent, which uses 32 watts. The shade will block a lot of the light. Notice that you can see through the shade on the thick piece of glass. (Even when switched off!)

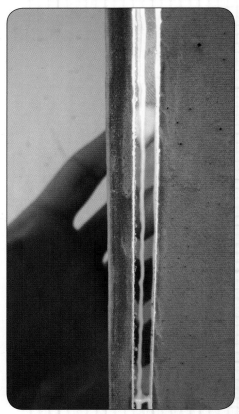

Road Sign Coffee Table

By William Holman (wholman)
(http://www.instructables.com/
id/Road-Sign-Coffee-Table/)

Road signs are a great material—strong, durable, weatherproof, and graphically interesting. I made this table out of two old signs; the legs came out of a sign that was 1' × 7', and the top was made from a sign that was 2' × 5'. Each is about thirty years old, which made the aluminum kind of brittle and prone to cracking on the bends. Basically, I drilled holes in the sign to weaken it, then hit it with a hammer while holding it against an edge to effect the folds. Again, because these signs were quite old, and not in the best condition, some cracking and breaking occurred. I also was pushing the bending radius and tightness of the folds, which obviously was pushing it a bit too far in some cases.

Lastly, these older signs are considerably thicker than newer ones, which I suspect also contributed to the deterioration of the seams. However, I still think the Instructable is valuable, in that this table is an experiment that enabled me to learn a lot about the material and the aesthetic possibilities of road signs.

I got the signs for free from some friends who inherited them with their apartment; other possible sources are junkyards, recycling centers, and eBay. Don't steal signs. Road signs are in place to protect people on the road; removing them illegally could have serious consequences, whether or not you get caught.

Since the signs were free, the only costs were drill bits and #8 machine bolts. I estimate the whole project was $10–$15. However, this method is pretty time consuming. Fortunately, it is the sort of thing that can be broken up over a series of weekends or nights. I took me a month of working in my spare time to make it—roughly twenty-five hours. Dimensions are all approximate, as I understand you may be trying to replicate this with different-dimensioned signs. The important thing to keep in mind is the overall ergonomics and human scale; a coffee table should sit no more than 17"–18" off the ground, and be at least 18" wide by whatever length the couch is.

Step 1: Model

I made some study models out of Bristol board to figure out my strategy. The photos are fairly self-explanatory as to the process. Making simple models to scale is a great way to think in 3D and figure out exactly how something might look and feel. The finished table does not strictly conform to this model, but it is very close. Use the dimensions of your sign and some cereal-box cardboard to come up with variations on folding strategies, leg configurations, and attachment schemes. Make several models, put them next to one another, and choose the one that looks the best and uses the available material most efficiently.

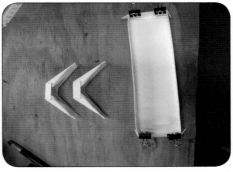

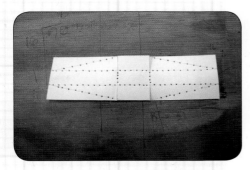

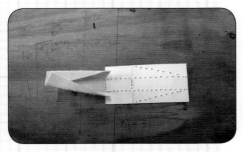

Step 2: Legs!

The legs are easier to make than they appear. Using an overall rectangle 12" × 18", two straight lines and two diagonal lines become folds; these folds eventually overlap one another to make a tapering form that can be pinned together with two machine bolts. The geometry is straightforward: Divide the piece lengthwise into three 4" × 18" strips. Run diagonals from two outside corners to the two middle lines. I laid it out in chalk; you can draw on the back with a Sharpie as well. Use a ⅛" drill bit to put pilot holes on one inch centers. Go back and drill every other one with a ¼" bit; get the alternating ones with a ⅜" bit. To bend, screw the sign down to a piece of wood through the smaller diameter holes, and hit with a mallet or small sledgehammer to achieve the bends. Once the two "wings" overlap, hammer them flat and clamp them together. Drill through with a ³⁄₁₆" drill bit and pin the metal together with #8 or #10 machine bolts and washers.

As you can see, these legs are asking a lot of the material. All four of them had at least some minor cracking. This can be avoided with newer, thinner signs; this table would also turn out quite well if executed in thinner sheet steel, as it isn't as tough to bend. Be careful not to cut yourself on the sharp edges of the aluminum; the shavings from the drilling make for nasty little splinters that are hard to see, hard to get out, and hurt a lot.

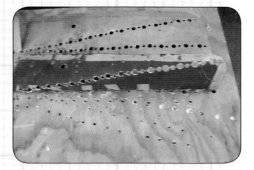

Step 3: Toppin'

The top is a 2' × 5' sign. On its own, this piece of metal was quite floppy. To stiffen it up and give two edges to bolt through, fold down a three-inch border on all four sides. Mark your lines, and then drill the holes in the same alternating pattern of diameters as you did for the legs. Make a slit with a hacksaw or an angle grinder in each corner, running at 45° from the outside corner to the intersection of the lines of holes. To bend, I put the line of holes on the edge of a curb and stood on the sign, then beat it with the hammer until

it was 90°. If the curb by your house is chamfered at an oblique angle, bend it as far as you can with that curb, then lay it down flat with the edges curled up. Lay a 2" × 4" along the seam and stand on that, then swing the mallet towards your legs to bend the sides upward. Clamp a block to the corners and curl the triangular flap in at each corner. The joinery and folding of the top is basically like wrapping a Christmas present.

As you can see in the photos, the two short end pieces broke off from the stress of the bends. One of the main reasons for that is the lever arm of the bend is only 3"; if the rim of the table was 10" or 12", there would be enough material to act as effective lever and peel up the bend. If they had stayed attached, the table would stronger and more stable. However, it is not a strict requirement that they be attached. The table is plenty strong with them being additive pieces; that said, try to avoid them breaking off if possible. As I said in the introduction, this is an experiment, and it is up to you to improve and expand this basic process.

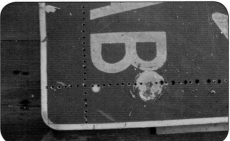

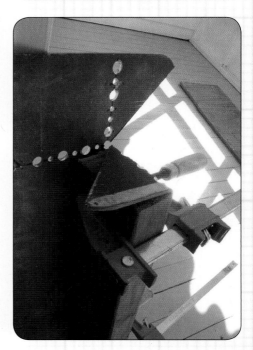

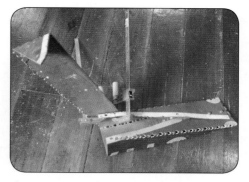

Step 4: Assembly

Now that you have a top and some legs, all that's left is to put them all together. It's pretty straightforward; three bolts go through the short side of the top into the side of the legs and two bolts go on the long side. Each bolt does double duty, securing the legs to the body of the table as well as securing the corner bends of the top to itself. Measure out a slope on the side pieces and mark with a Sharpie. Clamp in place, drill through, and tighten up. Run a level (or in this case, a 2" × 4" with a tiny combo square, because I don't have a long level) across the bottom of the legs to make sure the thing will sit flat when you're done. Repeat for all four legs. Flip it over and straight chill.

road sign coffee table

I recently moved into my first house and was in need of a dining room table. I saw a picture of a table that used an old section of bowling lane for its top and decided that I'd like to build something similar for myself. With about thirty hours of work over a few months, I was able to turn a tattered piece of wood into a beautiful, sturdy table that should never need replacement.

To find the lane section, I did a Craigslist search for bowling lanes and happened to find a guy about fifty miles away from me that was selling lane sections that he procured during a demolition job he was hired for. I paid about $300 for an 8' section with the arrow inlays. The section was about 2.5" thick and weighed about 250 pounds.

Step 1: Preparing the Lane

The first step in the process was to add support to the lane section to keep it from sagging. When the lanes are installed in the bowling alley, they are built in place. The builders lay down long strips of maple and side nail them to the adjacent maple pieces. No glue is used in the entire process, which means that, once the lane is taken up from the floor, it doesn't behave like a single slab of wood. All of the maple pieces are still tied together via the nails, but there is a certain amount of flex that the lane has. If not supported properly, the lane will sag quite dramatically in the middle due to its weight. To add support to the lane, I chose to inlay aluminum bars width-wise across the bottom of the table.

Using a hand router and a piece of metal to serve as a guide, I routed out three pockets across the width of the table. I made the pockets ¾" wide to accommodate the ⅝" aluminum square stock, and I made sure to make them a little deeper than necessary, because I needed to sand the bottom down and didn't want the belt of the sander to touch the metal pieces.

With the pockets routed, I set out drilling the aluminum bar stock. I spaced the holes so that each was centered with a piece of maple. The goal was to tie all of the pieces of maple together using the bar so that the table wouldn't sag in the future. When this was done, I ran screws through each hole and into the bottom of the table.

This resulted is a sturdy top that shouldn't sag.

top and bottom surfaces. Because the aluminum inlays on the bottom side were recessed, we were able to totally flatten that side out. If I hadn't recessed them, the shop said that they wouldn't have been able to sand that side. I felt that this was a great deal, because not only did the sanding come out perfect, but it saved me countless hours trying to recreate that process at home. I still had a little bit of hand sanding to do on the edges, but that was relatively easy compared to the top and bottom. I worked up to 220-grit sandpaper and called it good.

The lane was then ready for a few coats of polyurethane to seal it up. I used an oil-based polyurethane with a satin finish made by Minwax for the finish because I wanted to keep the natural color of the wood. I applied first to the bottom and sides of the lane, then I flipped it and did the top half. I applied about six coats in all, sanding with 220-grit sandpaper between each coat. The finish went on beautifully and I was really happy with the results.

Step 2: Sanding and Finishing the Lane

When I picked up the lane section from the seller, it was in pretty good shape, though the top was dirty and covered in decades of bowling alley oil, dirt, etc. I really wanted to sand a layer off the top to help clean it and a layer off the bottom to create a nice flat surface to mount legs to. I struggled with trying to decide the best way to sand the lane down and finally came across a local wood working shop that had a wide enough Timesaver belt sander. I brought the lane in on my day off and paid $60 to have them sand about ⅛" off of the

Step 3: Making the Legs

Because I don't really have a wood shop at home, I decided to have the legs CNC routed from 18mm-thick Baltic Birch plywood. This way all I had to do was glue the various sections together to make thicker sections, sand, and apply a finish, not to mention the neat tricks you can do with this type of manufacturing process, such as using slots as passages for bolts, creating pockets to keep weight down, and having overall accuracy, that make it possible to do things that would be more difficult using traditional woodworking methods.

I designed the legs using Solidworks and sent the files to a local CNC routing shop called RoboCut CNC. A few days later, I had the parts in hand and was ready to start gluing them together. I was amazed at how well the Baltic Birch cut. There wasn't any chipout on the edges and everything fit together perfectly.

To glue the parts together, I spread Titebond II wood glue on the faces to be glued and pressed them together using about eight C-clamps per part. Because alignment was critical, I included holes and pockets in all of the sections to accept two dowel pins. The dowels serve to align the sections together. This is important for looks, but also because I had several through holes that would need to accept hardware and, if those were misaligned, the hardware wouldn't fit correctly and could create an unsightly gap between the hardware and the wood.

The gluing went well, but there are some things I'd do differently next time. When pressure from the clamps is applied, some excess glue will squish out at the edges. My instinct was to wipe the glue off with a wet paper towel. Although this cleaned the bulk of the glue off, it also pressed a thin layer of glue into the pores on the edge of the wood. This created an ugly yellow glue smear that needed a lot of sanding time

to remove. Next time I would just let the glue be until it was dry and then remove it with a sharp chisel. This would have saved me lots of sanding time. Oh well.

With the legs glued together, it was time to apply a finish to them. By this time, it is really cold where I live, so applying finish in my unheated garage wasn't an option. Because of this, I needed to do the work in my basement, which meant that odor from the finish was a major concern. To cut down on the amount of VOCs in the air, I opted for a water-based polyurethane finish made by Minwax. The odor was almost nonexistent and I was happy with the results.

Step 4: Machining the Hardware

The table legs are built in several sections, which are then bolted together to form "trestle style" legs. To attach the sections together, I used cross dowels that I custom machined. They are made from 1.25" diameter aluminum round stock and there are twenty of them in total. These were part of a simple procedure that involved facing each piece to the right length (about 4.4"), putting a small chamfer on the edges using a file, slightly turning down the diameter to fit in the hole properly, and then drilling a tapping into a ⅜", 16 thread hole through the middle.

I had designed the holes in the wooden pieces to be slightly oversized by about 0.005"; however, I learned that the tolerance on the aluminum stock was slightly larger than expected so the aluminum stock would not fit in the holes as is. The benefit of this ended up being that I could get the fit of the hardware just right and that turning down the diameter left a nicer finish on the part.

Also, because of the gluing step for the wood, there was a little bit of glue residue left on the inside of the holes that the cross dowels needed to slide into. I hadn't counted on that and needed to get the glue out of there. To do this, I turned a tool on the lathe that was simply a long round piece of aluminum that had a diameter just slightly less than the diameter of the hole in the wood. I centered this in the hole and, with a few blows of the hammer, the tool was forced through the hole and sheared off any glue that was in there. The cross dowels were then machined slightly smaller in diameter than the tool; and, when slipped into place, everything fit perfectly.

Step 5: Assembly

This was the fun and easy part. Using the cross dowels and ⅜", 16 thread × 5" bolts (available at Home Depot) and some washers, I attached each section together until the table legs were standing. I also added some felt pads to the bottom of the table. It was pretty easy to do this by first assembling the legs and leg cross bars, and then adding the two long spanner pieces last. I had the table top resting on sawhorses that were slightly taller than the leg assembly. I slid the sawhorses to the extreme ends of the table top and was able to just slide the leg assembly underneath; then, I removed the sawhorses one by one so that the top was resting on the legs. Using some long screws, I was able to attach the top to the legs in a semi permanent way so that everything will break down easily for moving someday.

Wooden Candle Holder

By sam
(http://www.instructables.com/
id/Wooden-Candle-Holder/)

This is a handmade tea light holder, crafted from a log. I shaped a log from our firewood pile into a slab and drilled holes for the tea lights. It's pretty simple really, but the most important part is picking an attractive piece of wood and paying attention to nice finishing.

Tools

- A log shaping tool (band saw, hand saw, chainsaw, hatchet, plane, belt sander, mill, your teeth etc.)
- A large Forstner bit (either 1.5" or 1⅝")
- Drill
- Bike (optional)

Disclaimer: Use common sense or succumb to evolution.

on either side. It should be long enough for 1 to 100 candles, but I think odd numbers of candles looks best. I made two: one from option one and another from option three.

Option One: Take some firewood from your woodpile. Make sure it isn't rotten and that it doesn't have woodworm or other defects (unless you think they may look good).

Option Two: Go to a lumber yard or equivalent and tell them what you're trying to make; they can probably give you a scrap for very little or free.

Option Three: I met a tree surgeon who was working on a street near my house. I asked him for a fresh log that was in the back of his truck. I had to call him a number of times as he was an old guy who seemed to be hard of hearing—don't give up! He gave me a maple log for $2. Now, this is where the bike comes in. I was riding home when I met him, so I carried the log home bungee corded to my bike. Be careful, as it's impossible to steer and you become a very nice projectile.

Step 1: Acquiring Materials

For the wood, you have a couple of different options, but in general you want a hard wood (i.e., not pine 2" × 4") with nice grain and points of interest, like a knot or a rough edge with some bark. It can be any shape or size you like, as long as it is wide and deep enough to fit a tea light with a little extra space

Step 2: Shaping

Take a look at your piece of wood and search for your candle holder within the log. I kept one edge close to the edge of the log for bark and picked a length where there was a knot. To blank it out, you need one of the shapers mentioned earlier. I would suggest a saw, but I had a go with the hatchet for my firewood log attempt, which left the final piece more rustic, as there were deeper gouges from the hatchet. As you can see from the pictures, I made a cuboid, but you could make it any shape you like. Once you have the basic shape done, you can work on it with progressively finer tools—like a plane, then sander, then finer sandpaper. You should try using a plane if you haven't already—they are really fun, and they make a big mess of wood curls everywhere. A belt sander is really helpful, but not necessary. I put mine upside down in the vise so I could bring the work to the tool, not the other way round, which is easier for smaller stuff.

Step 3: Snack and Touchups

First things first, get something to eat, like a cup of tea and a cinnamon bun.

Look for any problem areas—where bark is lifting up, really big gouges, etc. For bark that's lifting up, fix it right away, because, when the break is fresh, the fibers connect back together better. Get some carpenter's glue and squidge it into the crack with your finger or a scrap piece of wood. Put a clamp on it and leave it to dry. If you made a big gouge, either make it part of the rustic look or fill it with wood filler. Follow the directions on the packet. Now you'll need to do more sanding to get rid of excess glue/filler. Doing lots of sanding with finer and finer grits is really worth it. Notice I'm sanding before drilling. The Forstner bits make a really clean cut into the piece, so it's easier to sand before you have holes to negotiate.

Step 4: Drilling Holes

Decide how many candles you want. For any odd number of candles, measure to the middle and place a mark; this is where you will drill for the middle candle. The rest of the marks are a little harder to explain, but you want an equal distance between the edges of your candles, not between centers, so you will need to know the radius of your drill bit. Then draw it around your drill mark with a compass.

Now you can measure from the edge. Position the remaining candles equal distances apart, and mark for holes. Or make a jig from scrap material, like I used for the firewood piece. First, drill a hole in a board for the jig, then move the edge of your jig to the edge of where you just drilled, and drill a hole through the hole in the jig. Keep moving it up, then cut off the end when you can't make any more holes. The most expensive part of this project was the Forstner bit, at around $30, but it's worth it to buy a quality tool. You can make lots more candle holders. I even have a few other projects that use the same bit. I found that a 1.5" Forstner bit was the largest Home Depot sells, but this only fits the tea light without the cup. If you want to fit the cup (which I suggest, so you don't set fire to the candle holder or have a waxy mess to scrape out), you will need a bigger size, which I found at an old school hardware store, Preston Hardware in Ottawa. They gave me a 1⅝", which fits the cup.

Note: All tea lights are not created equal. Mine are from IKEA. I found some others that are smaller and may fit into a 1.5" hole. Check what candles you have or can get before you buy a bit. If you have a drill press, this will be much easier. You can set the depth stop for the size of a candle. Then just start making wood chips. A hand drill would work okay, but clamp your piece securely and make sure you drill straight.

Step 5: Finish Up

If the edges of the holes are rough, give them a little sanding. Think about finishes—there are many you could do. My favorite is tung oil, which I used on the chopping board. I left the maple candle holder natural. I treated the longer log holder with liming wax, which brings out the grain in a big way. You could also stain it. Be careful about using potentially flammable finishes.

Buy some nice candles. I got beeswax tea lights from an environmental/organic shop called Arbour in Ottawa. They smell great. Wrap it up, and give someone a piece of firewood instead of a lump of coal. Now you've bought the expensive bit, make a few more or have a go at making a chopping board.

Simple Branching Coat Rack

By Sly Lee (slylee)
(http://www.instructables.com/
id/Simple-Branching-Coat-
Rack/)

This rack was inspired by a design I saw on Etsy. I do like to support local artists and craftsmen when possible, but at $75, this was not an option for me at the moment. In addition, I had a couple of extra branches and wood lying around. And, of course, as always, if it can be built, I will build it.

I have been teaching my girlfriend how to do basic handiwork, and for this project, I largely instructed and supervised while she assembled it. She did most of the sawing, nailing, and assembling.

- Saw
- Handsaw for cutting the branches
- Table saw, miter saw, chop saw, or handsaw to cut the frame

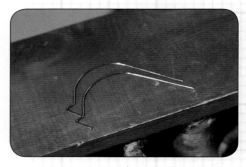

Step 1: Tools and Materials

The materials you will need will depend on how big and long you want your rack (or how much wood you have). I had enough wood to make a small one (15" long × 13" tall).
- ½" or ¾" plywood or hardwood
- Branching branches (I used 6.)
- Nails and/or screws (1" or so will do)
- 2 hanging hooks

Step 2: Step 1: Cut and Trim the Branches

Cut your branches to the appropriate height of your rack. I cut mine to be approximately 12". Trim the bottoms and tops of the branches if needed to make the branches stand upright. If you have a branch or two that has a weird lean or curve to it, leave it— it adds character. One of my branches had two branching sections (double the usage!). Also, if desired, trim the ends of the branching sections where your coat will hang.

Step 3: Cut the Boards for the Frame

Using your miter, table, chop, or handsaw, cut the boards to make the frame. My frame was approximately 8" deep, 15" long, and 13" tall.

Step 4: Attach Branches to the Frame

Using nails or screws, attach the branches to the bottom of the frame first (or the top; the order doesn't matter). If you are using screws, it may be useful to pre-drill the holes first.

Step 5: Finish the Frame and Secure Branches

After you have attached your branches to the bottom of the frame, attach the sides of the frame using screws or nails. Then attach the top of the frame. Secure the top of the branches to the frame with nails or screws.

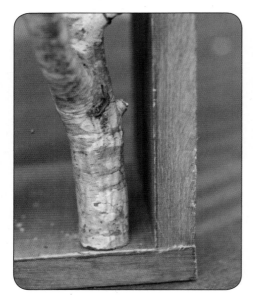

The wood I used was already quite old, so I didn't have to do anything.

Hang it up using the two hanging hooks (you know the "As Seen on TV" hooks). I found they are actually pretty useful and durable, especially when you don't have any studs.

Besides a rack, this also serves as a shelf! This is a small prototype. Later on, I may build a longer one.

Step 6: Finishing touches

Sand off any protruding edges. Use wood sealant or varnish to protect your new coat rack. If you want a "vintage" look to it, you could try putting some dents in the side with a hammer or nail.

Want a DIY way to cook food *without* using fossil fuel LP or having to buy charcoal? I know I did. That's why I built a rocket grill! This is just one variation of a "rocket stove"—a simple appropriate technology for cleanly burning bio-fuels.

The rocket grill is fired by twigs, wood scraps, wood chips, or nearly anything else you can put in it. It naturally drafts air to maximize combustion. Once the grill is really going, no smoke comes out the top, only heat, and the grill really does sound like a rocket!

The grill is designed to not only grill, but also boil, bake, braise, and roast! Because of the simple design and robust construction, it is nearly maintenance free. Unlike an LP grill, the burner will never burn and rust away to nothingness (and cost good time and money to replace). There is no piezo-electric starter or other "modern" technology in the grill, which would be prone to failure.

Despite how it looks, the grill is small and light enough for one grown man to lift into the back of a pickup truck. That way, you can travel with it for camping or tailgating. (The lid and side tables are also removable for storage and easy packing.) Because it's covered and enclosed, it also qualifies for use as a "backyard fire-pit" in areas that do not allow open fires.

This project is mostly simple metal work. While it does require welding, it's pretty straight forward. This was really my first-ever welding project. So let's gather together our tools and materials and get started!

Step 1: Tools and Materials

Tools

- Angle grinder
- Grinding disc
- Cut-off disc
- Welder
- Safety glasses, work gloves, welding gloves, welding helmet, hearing protection
- Drill and drill bits
- Laser level, bubble level (optional)

Materials

This project is made mostly from scrap metal but will need several other parts.

Parts for the Grill Itself

- A base or something for the grill to stand on. Must be heatproof. I used a scrap steel farm implement disc.

- Steel pipe—diameter of your choice, but it will affect cooking size and fuel rate. I used 6.5" diameter scrap steel pipe, about 3' in length.
- Steel water tank (This becomes the "bowl" top of the grill and cooking surface area.)
- 4 pieces of small diameter steel pipe, about 6" in length
- 2 90° pipe elbows of same diameter
- 2 pipe flanges of same diameter
- 2 pieces of flat material that you like to make side countertop surfaces
- Small scraps of steel plate

Parts for the Lid of the Grill
- A piece of wood, species of your choice, sized for a lid handle
- 2 carriage bolts (about 5" long) with matching nuts and washers. Stainless steel is ideal, as these will be exposed to both heat and the elements. Plain steel is fine as a lower cost alternative.
- 2 pieces of copper or steel tube or pipe, slightly larger diameter and shorter length than the carriage bolts, to use as spacers
- The top end of the water tank

Other Items
- Steel plate, about 6" side × 12" long (perforations or slotted is ideal)
- JB Weld epoxy

First, gather together your materials for the main section of the rocket grill.
- Base
- Large diameter pipe
- Water tank

The base needs to be large enough to keep the whole grill from tipping over. It also forms the very end bottom of the grill, which hot coals and ashes will fall into. Any sort of steel plate would work fine. I found a piece of old farm machinery that fit the bill. It's a domed disc about 16" in diameter.

The large diameter pipe needs to be cut into two sections. Make one about

1', and the other about 20" long. The 20" section will be the "vertical tube," and the 1' section will be the "feeder tube."

That water tank that I chose was 16" in diameter. It was already cut apart from a solar water experiment I worked on. The bottom section of the tank is cut to about 1' tall. This becomes the cooking area "bowl" top to the grill. The water tank was also chosen because it is large enough in diameter to fit my camping cast iron Dutch oven and a stock pot that I use for boiling corn.

Stacked up, the base, vertical tube, and water tank section should come to a comfortable standing height for you. The top of the water tank section is the height that grilling will take place.

To cut the steel, I found that an angle-grinder with a cut-off disc works best. I made cuts quickly, without removing to much metal, and made a nice, straight line. You could also use a reciprocating saw with a metal cutting blade or a plasma-cutter if you have access to one.

To mark a line on a cylindrical object like the pipe or water tank, wrap a straight section of sheet metal around it, and secure with masking or duct tape. Mark this line with a permanent marking pen, then remove the sheet metal.

Cut the pipes and water tank to length, using common-sense safety precautions. (Wear work gloves, eye and hearing protection, etc.) Cut the top off the water tank and save to make the lid.

Stack up the base, vertical pipe, and water tank section to get a feel for how your grill will look. If you were working on a level surface, like a concrete garage floor, you can use a bubble level to make sure your vertical pipe is perfectly straight up and down. (Plumb!)

of an angle will not allow for proper air-flow and can prevent the grill from drafting properly.

Cutting the two pipes to fit together can be geometrically-challenging. An angle-grinder makes straight cuts, but both pipes are rounded. Still, they have to meet together tight enough to get a good weld between them. What you need to do is imagine how two straight cuts would look projected onto two curved surfaces. One easy way to do this is to use a laser level that has the ability to project a straight line. Several inches up from the end, point the laser at the vertical pipe, at the angle you want the feeder pipe to meet it. Then mark the laser line with your permanent marker. Rotate the laser 90° and mark the line again.

On the feeder pipe, mark two lines at 90° from each other the same way. Another way to mark the same cuts is to use sheet metal, which you can wrap around the pipes. It is possible to make a projection of what the cuts should look like, and cut that out of the sheet metal. Then wrap the sheet metal around the pipe and mark it. A friend of mine already had made a sheet metal template, so that's the technique I used.

When you are done, you will have a notch in the vertical pipe and a "bird's beak" cut in the feeder pipe. Fit the two pipes together, and see how close they match up. It's more that likely that you will need to use a grinder to get the parts to fit together well.

Step 2: The Special Cut

The most distinct feature of the Rocket Grill is how the feeder pipe and vertical pipe come together. While the exact angle that they connect at isn't super important, it should be somewhere between 90° and 45°. Having this connection at some angle makes it easier to feed fuel and prevents it from bending over too far. Too steep

Step 3: Welding

Weld together the vertical and feeder pipes. That's easiest to do with both pipes lying flat and sideways. Weld around one side, then flip it over, and weld the other side.

Next, stand the Y of pipes on top of the base. Make sure it is centered and that it is plumb and level. Weld the pipes to the base. (Make sure to always brush down the metal where you will be welding, and where the ground clamp connects.)

The bottom of the water tank needs a hole cut in it, the same diameter as the vertical pipe. Mark that diameter hole on the bottom. One way to do that is just set the other parts right on top of the tank and trace it. Then cut the hole in the bottom of the tank. I had a plasma-cutter at a friend's house, so I used that. Otherwise, a cut-off disc, Sawzall, or large diameter hole-saw could work.

Stack the whole grill together upside down and weld the vertical tube to the water tank section. Again, make sure the parts are plumb and level. If there is a "front" to the water tank, make sure it's where you want it to be. On mine, there were two pipe ports that I wanted to be left and right, with the feeder tube on an angle to my right as I faced it.

At this point, the basic grill is done, but we still need the lid and a few other details.

Step 4: Fuel/Air Plate

Another distinct feature of the Rocket Grill is the fuel/air plate. It holds the fuel up and in place, and it allows plenty of air to naturally draft into the grill and up through the fuel for a very hot and clean burn. The plate needs to be able to hold up to high temperatures.

Take some scrap steel plate and cut it to a width just slightly smaller than the diameter of the feeder pipe and about the same length. This way, the plate sits *inside* the feeder pipe and divides it to an upper and lower area. Fuel goes in *above* the plate and air goes in *below* the plate. The plate has holes or slots in it in the far end so that it supports the fuel but allows plenty of air through. The plate I used was already slotted, but I added a few more for good measure. You could also use a heavy-duty grate, or weld together re-bar to serve the same purpose. When you are ready, just slide the plate into the feeder tube. Gravity and friction will hold it in place for you.

Step 5: Building the Lid

When I cut the water tank apart, I also cut off the top and saved it for use as a lid. It's already the same diameter as the top of the grill, so it should fit perfect. It really just needs two modifications: a handle and a way to let air through.

The Handle

The length and width of the handle is based on the size of the user's hand, preferably with enough room for an oven mitt. I found a scrap of oak firewood, about the right diameter for a handle, and left it long to start with. I could always shorten it later. Drill two holes in the wood, and push the carriage bolts through. Use these to mark where they should go through on the lid. Drill two holes in the lid.

Cut two sections of pipe a little shorter than the length of the carriage bolts. These will be spacers to hold the handle the right distance from the lid. I had some scrap copper pipe around, which is easy to cut and looks very nice. Slide a washer and then the pipe over the carriage bolts, and then place the carriage bolts into the holes in the lid. On the bottom side of the lid, attach washers and nuts and tighten.

Air Spacers

The lid also needs some way for hot air to constantly exit the grill to continue the chimney effect. You could make a vent, similar to one like a Weber brand grill or even some sort of chimney right on the lid, but it seemed much easier just to add some small steel tabs. These tabs space the lid away from the grill to allow air flow. I cut three steel tabs from scrap metal and welded them evenly around the lid.

On the inside of the grill, I welded in three matching tabs that line up with the ones on the lid. Three tabs keep the lid from wobbling. By simply rotating the lid a little, it can still sit all the way down on the grill (such as when you are done with the grill and want to smother it or for storage).

Step 6: Side Tables

What's a grill without some workspace to hold your utensils, your plate of meat, and your favorite beer? That's why the grill needs side tables.

The water pressure tank used to make the top of the grill included pipe connections in the sides. I purchased just a couple short sections of pipe and elbows so that these could support the side tables. I threaded in a horizontal pipe into each side, and then I inserted a 90° elbow into that. A vertical pipe section then completes an L on either side of the grill.

Both side tables have a pipe flange going to a short piece of pipe smaller in diameter than the vertical side pipe. That way, the side table pipe sits inside the vertical pipe. This makes it easy to remove the side tables for travel. Drilling a hole through both pipes allows me to slide a small bolt through, preventing the side table from accidentally rotating.

At first, I wasn't sure what I wanted to use for the top surface of the side tables. I dug through my pile of scrap/salvaged/recycled materials and found an assortment of stone, tile, steel, aluminum, and wood. I simply set different pieces of materials on top of the side-arm pipes to see what looked good. In the end, I decided on a blue/green slate stone for the left side, and a steel deck place for the right side.

For the steel on the right, I just welded the pipe flange to the bottom of it, threaded in the short section of pipe, and slid that into the slightly larger diameter vertical pipe. A horizontally-drilled hole with a bolt slid through it completed that side.

The slate for the left was a little more work. The slate was rough and pointed, but it is a very soft stone. I experimented and found that rubbing the edges of the stone with a cold chisel allowed me to shape the stone a bit and smooth the rough edges.

To attach the stone to the side pipe, I found some scrap metal about the right size for the bottom of the stone side table. I welded the pipe flange to the bottom of the metal and then glued that to stone with a tube of JB WELD adhesive. Again, the pipe on the side table just slides into the vertical pipe on the side of the grill.

Step 7: Odds and Ends

Paint Removal

The water tank section of the grill is painted, and the paint had to be removed before using the grill for cooking. I thought about what the most "eco-friendly" way to remove all the paint was. I thought about all the nasty chemicals used as paint strippers. In the end, I decided make a very hot test fire to both try out the grill and remove the paint. The paint easily peeled off.

Pot Bracket

To hold either the stock pot or Dutch oven, there still needs to be air space in the bottom of the grill. The easiest answer was just to span the fire tube with two short sections of slotted C-channel. They support the pot and let plenty of heat and air through. They are not welded in place. I didn't see any reason to, and this way they are removable.

Heat Diffuser

One downside of this grill design is that it gets an extreme hot-spot in the middle of the grill and is much cooler towards the outside edge. That's a bad thing for cooking burgers and sausages. So I put in a "heat diffuser" when grilling. It's just a small steel plate that I practiced welding on before welding the grill together. It simply sits directly on the pot bracket and works well to spread out the heat. At some point, I may make a more aesthetically-pleasing heat spreader, but this one works fine for now.

Ash Cleanout

You may have noticed that there is no ash cleanout on the grill. In truth, I really haven't seen a design for one that I like. I have seen similar steel rocket stoves that use a threaded pipe port, which seems like it would gunk up the threads easy. Also a large diameter pipe port gets expensive quickly, and I was trying to use as many free, inexpensive, and recycled parts as possible. For now, I just flip the whole grill upside down to empty the ash. It makes far less ash than you might think. In the future, I may use the angle grinder to cut an angle out of the bottom back side of the grill and then hinge it, so that there is a flip-up flap to access and empty the ash.

Grill Grate

The grate is just a standard round grill grate. It's the medium size. It actually overlaps the top of the grill, which makes it easier to use the entire top. Downside? It's easier to slide a burger right off the top of the grill as well!

corn on the cob, or whatever I am going to cook up next.

To start the grill, I just put a little bit of tinder (usually a bit of newspaper) and a few twigs onto the far end of the fuel/air plate. I light it with a match or cigarette lighter and then just feed in a few more twigs. After that, a fair amount of sticks, firewood, or other fuel can be loaded on the top side of the fuel plate.

The fire is very simple to light and starts right up. Even *extra long* fuel can go right in. Just slide it a little farther in every once in a while. The chimney effect makes all the heat go up the vertical tube. No smoke or fire comes out the feeder tube.

I am right-handed, so I designed the grill so that the feeder tube comes out on an angle to the right. That way, it is easy for me to fuel, but I don't hit my shin on it. Since pots sit down inside the grill when boiling, the heat transfer of the fire to the pot is very good. The heat hits not just the bottom of the pot but travels up the sides as well. This means you get a boil going faster, while using less fuel.

I also used my grill in a rain storm a while back. My concern was rain running down the lid and then inside the grill. It wasn't an issue—any rain hitting the lid simply vaporized or sizzled right off!

Step 8: Fueling and Firing

One of the best things about the Rocket Grill is how it's fueled. No longer do I have to purchase fossil-fuels to cook my backyard fare! Because of the amount of air that flows through the grill, almost any bio-fuel burns great in it. This one is really designed for twigs and sticks.

After every wind storm, all of my neighbor's trees shed their sticks downwind into my yard. Before, I would grumble at the yard-work of picking up all those sticks and moving them back to the brush pile. Now, I instead gather them up looking forward to burgers,

Step 9: Grill It Up!

So far, I have used the grill for chicken, burgers, brats and sausages, corn on the cob, shish kebab, and more. The design also allows me to boil in the stock pot or bake in the Dutch oven. (I'm working on baked desserts now, too!)

A friend of mine has designed both a giant skillet and a very nice wok for his. Another possible future modification is to create a high-thermal mass pizza oven top for the grill.

Rocket stoves lend themselves well to infinite variation and re-use of existing materials. Combine that with versatility and efficient use of fuel, and you have the cook stove of tomorrow, today.

Remember, this isn't rocket science, just good use of appropriate technology! I hope you find my Rocket Grill to be inspirational. You too can cook net-carbon-zero deliciousness over open flames and take pride in your own design.

Bentwood Birdhouse

By rabbitcreek
(http://www.instructables.com/
id/Bentwood-Birdhouse/)

Building birdhouses is one of those classic things to do with your hands. We are first exposed to the process in high school wood class. Frustrating moments with poorly fitting plywood and nails usually end any interest in the project. This is a new twist on the design for these usually dull construction projects that will actually look good on the outside of your house this summer and involves fun construction techniques uncommon for this type of project. The process uses bendable poplar wood plywood that is made in Italy and is available at most specialty wood shops, assembled in a composite epoxy-coated structure that is light, waterproof, and elegant.

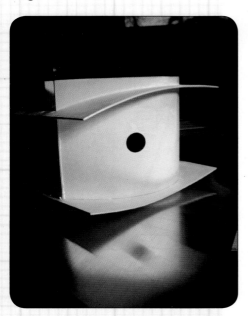

Step 1: Tools and Materials
- Bendable poplar plywood 4" × 8" sheet—about $35
- West System 105-B Epoxy Resin 32 ounces
- West System 206-B Slow Hardener 27 ounces
- Foam brushes
- Craftsman or RotoZip cutter tool with ⅛" rotary blade for wood
- Razor blade knife with utility blade
- Shirt cardboard, four pieces 8" × 12"
- Elmer's carpenter's wood filler—interior/exterior
- Hot glue gun
- Sandpaper or sanding block
- Bits: ¼" and 1.5"
- Clamps

Step 2: Modeling the Birdhouse

This birdhouse design is a simple arrangement of four pieces of 8" × 12" bendable poplar plywood. I began with a model of the construction made up of four pieces of shirt cardboard—a construction material that I remember fondly from my childhood. These are still available from your shirts if you have them boxed and laundered; otherwise you can cut them out of "store bought" cardboard. The roof and the floor consist of identical cut designs that hold the curved sides in place. The curved cuts in the cardboard model should be centered mirror images of each other and should not extend further than ½" from the edges of the cardboard. The type of curve you draw and model are up to you, but the curve must be long enough to accommodate the length of the side pieces. In the model, you can cut the slits with a razor-knife; in the poplar you will be cutting the slits with a ⅛" RotoZip bit that will allow the plywood to slip in.

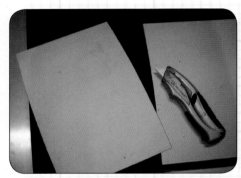

Step 3: Cutting the Pieces

There is a natural curve to the panel of plywood, and the four identical pieces of poplar plywood required in each birdhouse all should curve in their long dimension. The 8" × 12" pieces can be easily marked out on the large sheet so that you should get six pieces out of the 48" side of the sheet. The plywood is easily cut with a straightedge and a razor knife.

Step 4: Drawing the Cuts

The inspiration for the design of the birdhouse came from a wing shape that I had in my mind. I used a curve tool to get the shape I wanted and cut a piece of wood to use in tracing the line on the poplar plywood pieces. The lines were drawn so that they stopped ½" from the ends of the plywood and were mirrored across the long axis of the piece, staying 1" away at the ends. Other similar cuts can work and you can experiment with the design. Both the roof and the floor piece are drawn out in the exact same way.

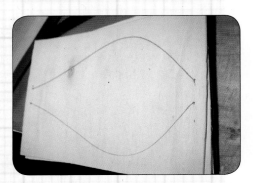

Step 5: Cutting the Groove

I usually cut both marked top and bottom at one time—if building multiple houses you can cut four of these sheets at one time. It is best to clamp the sheets securely before cutting. I drill start and stop holes at the end of each line with a ¼" bit and then proceed to cut out the long channels with the RotoZip or Craftsman equivalent rotary drill with the ⅛" bit. This will form the tight slot that will hold the wall pieces in place. It takes a little practice to get a smooth cut, but, if you are moving slowly, the line will be quite steady. This is an amazing piece of technology and useful for a lot of other projects.

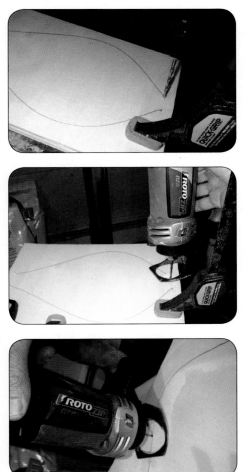

Step 6: Cut the Bird Hole

I used a 1.5" bit to cut this—the literature varies on this dimension and I won't get into it. The hole should be cut about halfway up the side in the portion which curves the least—you don't want to press your luck when you are bending this stuff; holes definitely weaken it. Only one of the side pieces gets a hole!

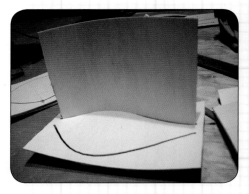

Step 7: Assembly

This is the fun part. This takes a little goofing with, but with a bit of gentle bending, you can get all the pieces together. Get the top or bottom on first and then move it down on the pieces to stabilize it before putting on the opposite one. After getting it roughly together, carefully adjust the top and bottom to match the wing-shaped curves of the sides.

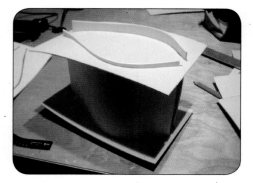

Step 8: Sealing It Up

Measure the openings on the two ends and cut side pieces to fit in these spaces out of the poplar plywood. The structure can be temporarily tacked together with a few dots of hot glue. The side and the top are self-tensioning and usually don't require this—only the end pieces do.

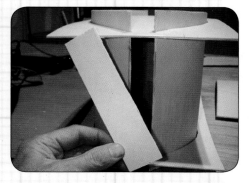

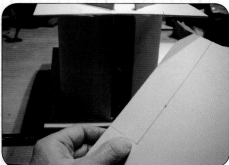

the two components and to apply it to the structure. Not only does it glue the whole thing together into a composite structure, it also forms a weather barrier to keep it going for many summers to come. Make sure you treat the end cuts of all the plywood. The stuff hardens overnight, and you'll have at least twenty minutes to put it on. Make sure you get the stuff into the cracks to glue and seal them. Only one coat of epoxy is necessary to seal and glue the structure. Wear latex gloves for this step.

Step 9: Epoxy Coating

The West System is very nice. It usually includes the self measuring pumps attached to the hardener and the epoxy. If you haven't used epoxy systems before, you should read up on safety rules that come with the stuff. It is really easy to use and it takes about six pumps of each one to make a large enough batch to coat the whole structure. You use a sponge brush to mix

Step 10: Sealing and Sanding

There will be some openings in the structure once the epoxy dries. Seal these with some wood filler of the appropriate color. The structure can then be sanded to smooth out the small defects that occur when applying epoxy for the first or fortieth time. The final structure can then be left a natural color by applying a polyurethane finish or an appropriate outdoor paint.

Step 11: Ready for the Birds

You may want to modify the design so you are able to remove one of the small end panels for cleaning between residents. You can also cut the square edges off with your rotary cutter tool. These structures are very fun to make, and modeling them with cardboard can get you a neat lunchbox or a variety of other bendable composite creations.

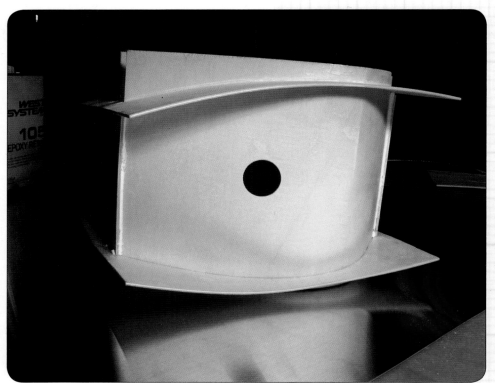

Paracord Bracelet with a Side Release Buckle

By Stormdrain
(http://www.instructables.com/id/Paracord-bracelet-with-a-side-release-buckle/)

This tutorial will show how to make a paracord bracelet with a side release buckle. When made on a larger scale, you can make this for use as a dog or cat collar as well. A reliable online source for paracord is the Supply Captain; for side release buckles, check out Creative Designworks.

Step 1: Materials
- Paracord or equivalent ⅛" diameter cord
- A tape measure or ruler
- Scissors
- Side release buckle
- A lighter (torch lighter works best)

The amount of cord used can vary, but for this example, we'll use 10' of paracord to start with. Actual amount of cord used for the bracelet is about 1' of cord for every 1' of knotted bracelet length. So if your wrist is 8", you'd use approximately 8' of cord.

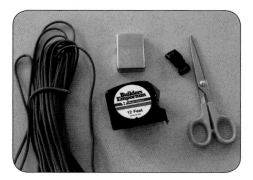

Step 2: Measure Wrist

Wrap the paracord around you wrist and make a note of where the cord meets. Hold this point next to your ruler or tape measure and that's your wrist size.

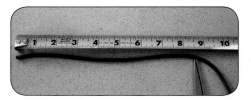

Step 3: Find the Center of the Cord

Hold the ends of the cord together and find the center of the loop. Take the center of the cord and pull it through one end of the buckle (either side of the buckle, it doesn't matter). Now pull the cord ends through the loop until it's tightened up and attached to the buckle.

You're measuring from the end of the female part of the buckle to the flat part of the male end of the buckle. (The part with the prongs doesn't count for the measurement because the prongs fit inside the female part of the buckle when the bracelet is closed.)

Step 4: Finding the Bracelet Length

Take the buckle apart and pull the free ends of the cord through the other part of the buckle, sliding it up towards the attached part. You're going to measure the distance between the two buckle ends for the bracelet size for your wrist. Add about 1" to your measured wrist length—this will make the finished bracelet a comfortable fit.

Step 5: Start Making the Knots

The knot used for the bracelet has a few different names—cobra stitch, Solomon bar, and Portuguese sinnet. Take the cord on the left side and place it under the center strands running between the buckle ends. Now take the cord on the right side under the left side cord, over the center strands, and through the loop of the left side cord. Tighten up the cords so the half knot you just formed is next to the buckle. Now take the right side cord under the center strands. The left side cord goes under the right side cord, over the center strands, and thru the loop of the right side cord. Tighten up the cords (not too tight, just until they meet the resistance of the knot) and now you have a completed knot. You will continue doing this, alternating the left and right sides as you go. If you don't alternate, you'll quickly see a twisting of the knots; just undo the last knot and alternate it to correct.

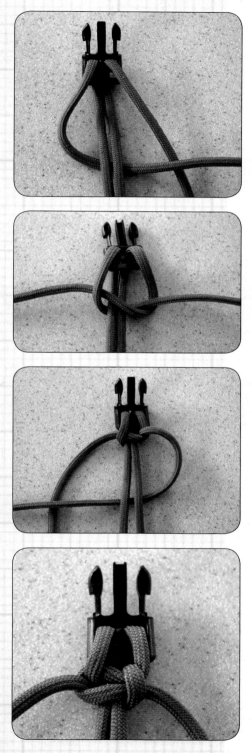

Step 6: Continue knotting

Keep tying the knots until you have filled the space between the buckle ends. The knots should be uniform from one end to the other. Tie each knot with the same tension to keep them all the same size.

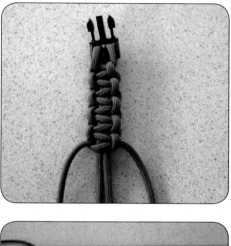

Step 7: Trim the Excess Cord and Melt the Ends

You can now use your scissors to trim off the extra cord closely to the last knot you tied. I trim one at a time, and use my lighter to quickly melt the end I cut, wait a second for the melted cord to cool just a bit and then use my thumb to press the melted end onto the surrounding cord so it hardens as it attaches. You must be careful with this step. The melted cord is extremely hot, and it's possible to get burned, so you might also try using a soldering iron or wood burning tool for the melting step if you wish, or even use something like a butter knife or the knurled section of a tool to flatten out the melted end of the cord to finish it.

An alternative to melting the ends is to tuck/pull the ends under the last couple of knots. I have used hemostats to do this on the inside of the bracelet then trimmed them to finish. It does work and is just barely noticeable as the cords add a slight bulge at that end of the bracelet.

Step 8: You're Finished

If you did everything correctly, it should look something like the finished one below. Once you know what you're doing, you can vary the amount of cord used by making the knots tighter or looser and pushing the knots closer together as you go can use more cord.

A tip for paracord bracelets: If the side release buckle is large enough, you can loop the paracord around them again before you start knotting, to fill in the extra room on the buckle. The ½" side release buckles are a tight fit for this but will work, and the ⅝" size are just right. This leaves a two-strand core for the bracelet when you start knotting. Now, you could also have a four strand core by starting with a lark's head on the first buckle end, using a double wrap on the second buckle end (at your wrist size), running the cord back to and over the first buckle end, then knotting over the four-strand core.

Or, for a six strand-core, lark's head first buckle, run the two strands around the second buckle (at your wrist size), back to and around the first buckle (now has four strands around), then back to and around the second buckle, and start knotting around the six core strands. This gives extra cord in case you need it for whatever, but it also makes the paracord bracelets thicker and more rounded, which I personally didn't care for.

Step 9: Other Variations

Once you have the hang of the basic bracelet/collar, you can add another layer of cobra stitches overlapping first set of knots, called a king cobra stitch/doubled Solomon bar/doubled Portuguese sinnet. The amount of cord used for a king cobra is about twice as much as for the regular stitch. Glow-in-the-dark cord can be found at CoolGlowStuff.com. Both the 1/16" and 3/32" sizes work well for the bracelets and can be used alone or combined with paracord.

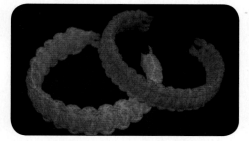

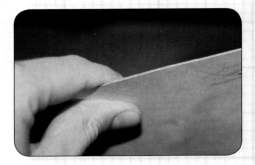

This Instructable will show you how to make a simple wood ring.

Materials:

* Piece of wood veneer, approximately 6" × 6"
* Wood glue
* Food coloring
* Clear nail polish

Tools:

* Scissors
* Drill
* Band saw
* ⅝" drill bit
* Belt sander or sandpaper

Approximate time: 1 to 2 hours of work and about two nights of drying time for wood glue and dyes.

Step 1: Cutting the Chips

Use heavy-duty scissors to cut chips that are about 1" on both sides. This ring has a thickness of 6 chips, but, depending on the veneer you use and the desired thickness, you can adjust accordingly.

Step 2: Dyeing the Wood

This step is optional. I've made rings in the past without dye. For those, I use a wood burner on low to give the ring a slightly rustic look and polish. That aesthetic is more appealing to me, but I'll include the directions for the colored ring since it is more complicated.

Using a glass dish, mix a strong dye out of water and food coloring and let the chips soak in it overnight. I chose pink and teal for these chips—three of each color. After about eight hours, rinse the chips and let them dry completely.

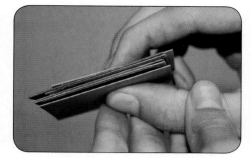

Step 3: Making the Ply

These veneers will be glued together to make a very thin, strong plywood. Decide on a design for the ring, based on your colors, alternating the grain of the wood to make the ply stronger. Between each layer of wood, lay down a thin, even layer of wood glue, then clamp it all in place between two spare pieces of wood.

Step 4: Shaping the Ring

Choose a drill bit that is slightly narrower than the diameter of your finger. This will allow you to sand the inside of the ring smooth. I've found that a ⅝" bit generally works for an average finger. Drill a pilot hole, and then the final hole, making sure to leave room around the edges for the ring itself.

Then, use a band saw to carefully cut out the rough shape of your ring, leaving it slightly larger than desired so that it can be sanded smooth.

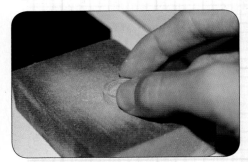

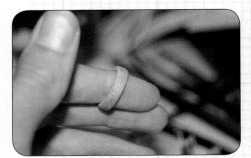

Step 5: Finishing the Ring

Using a belt sander or rough sandpaper, sand the ring to its desired shape and size. The ply is quite strong, so don't worry too much about keeping it thick for strength's sake. Then hand-sand the ring using a fine sandpaper (something around 400 should be the last sanding). Now finish the ring. The finish should offer an aesthetic as well as functional purpose. For the colored ring, I liked something clear and shiny, so I used a hard clear nail polish. For the non-colored ring, this is when I would lightly burn the wood.

Step 6: Finished Ring

Once the finish is dry, the ring is done!

Build a Programmable Mechanical Music Box

By Matt Bechberger
(mattthegamer463)
(http://www.instructables
.com/id/Build-a-Programmable-
Mechanical-Music-Box/)

Have you ever seen those little music boxes you wind up, or crank, that play a little tune over and over from a little metal drum of notes, and wished they did more than play the same ten-second tune over and over for eternity? If only you could change the song and write your own music for it. . . . Now there's an idea.

After a year of design and work, I completed my Re-Programmable Music Box/Mechanical Synthesizer/Organ Grinder Thingy. It has many names, and is 100 percent non-electric. Just wood, metal, and good ol' people power.

I began this project as a sort of proof-of-concept, designing something from scratch without a lot to base it off of, and a whole lot of engineering problems to solve. Also, I didn't really know what I was doing. It was intended to be a learning and problem-solving experience. And it was a lot of fun.

Step 1: Design and Planning

Since I was starting this project entirely from scratch, I needed to make a flawless design that could be easily worked with, and a good design always reduces waste. I decided to use oak and, at $60 per a 10' plank, I didn't want to waste any. Also, it's pretty complex and precision is extremely important for everything to work correctly.

I started with this idea: a large wooden cylinder will hold metal pegs. It will rotate and force the pegs to pluck metal tines, which are tuned to specific notes.

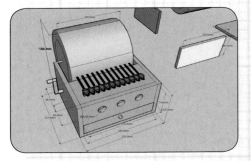

I selected twelve notes across, since it seemed like a very flexible number of notes and allowed me to fill it with a simple eight-note scale in the middle, with a few extra high and low notes. I could also tune in flats or sharps, if I wanted some specifically, or get almost all of a chromatic scale in. I selected thirty-two notes "around" the cylinder, because that's what you need to play Pop Goes The Weasel, or any eight-bar song using quarter notes.

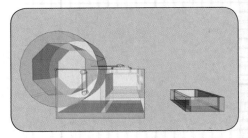

The cylinder is made of softwood, 8" in diameter, that I picked up from a nearby carpenter for free. I found a belt that fit snugly around it to use along with a few gears and a belt for the cranking mechanism.

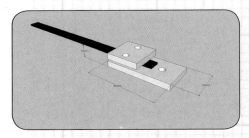

The tine material was cut from the prongs of a garden rake. This works great because it is flexible but snaps right back into place. The tine holder design was sort of up in the air until the rest of the machine was done, so that I could do testing. Initial designs were too complex and tiny, but the final design is about as simple as possible, I believe.

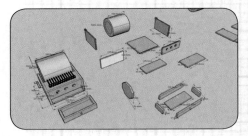

Originally I wanted to use almost all wood for this project, but it turned out wood wasn't going to offer the precision that I needed for the tines. I ended up doing it with a CNC at my college. In Step 7, I hypothesize how it could be accomplished without such expensive tools.

When designing the wooden frame, try to place the pieces to get as few exposed edges as possible. For the edges you do have, try to align them so that they create borders and still look appealing to the eye.

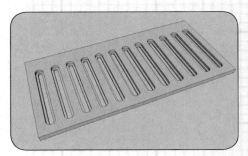

Step 2: Materials and Tools

Materials:

- Oak plank (10' long × 8" wide × ¾" thick is what I started with)
- 8" long × 8" diameter wood cylinder
- Aluminum plate
- 1" wide ¼" thick aluminum stock
- 100 steel pegs
- 384⅛" diameter × ⅛" long magnets
- Rake tines
- 8" rubber belt
- Smaller belt
- 3 gears
- Carriage bolt and nut
- ~12" long ¼" steel rod
- ¼" wooden dowel
- Biscuits
- Instrument mallet

Tools:

- Table saw
- Band saw
- Drill press
- Number drill set
- Fractional drill set
- Wood glue
- Clamps
- Drill bits
- Biscuit cutter
- Planer
- 1" hole saw
- Polyurethane wood sealant
- Pliers

Note: I'm going to assume you know how to use your planer, your table saw, your band saw, your drill press, etc., and I won't go into detail about the operation of the machines. If you're using someone else's machines, have them teach you how to use them and have someone around for safety.

Step 3: Woodwork—Part 1

So it's tough to find wood in the shapes you want at the lumber store, so I bought a 10' long piece that was only 8" wide. My solution was to chop it into three 3.3' segments and glue them together to form a 2' × 3.3' oak board.

First, chop the plank into three even pieces. Then, plane them down to ½" thickness, since ¾" is too thick for such a small project. Next, cut biscuit notches with the biscuit cutter and glue them in place. Be sure to mark the locations of the biscuits so that you can plan around them, so they won't be visible after making cuts. Clamp it together and let it dry for twenty-four hours.

Measure the circumference of the cylinder, and divide it by thirty-two. Mark thirty-two lines all the way around the cylinder. Now, mark twelve holes along each line for each note. There should be 384 points to drill now.

To drill the cylinder, set a vice on the drill press bed and put a few rags inside the open jaws so that the wood won't get damaged. Use a weight on a string to check that the line of holes you are drilling are straight and vertical. Find a number drill that is a few thousandths of an inch larger than ⅛" and drill the holes exactly 1" deep using the depth control on the press.

Next, glue a magnet into the bottom of each hole. This is to prevent the pegs from falling out when the drum holds them upside down. The best way to do this is to place a magnet on the end of a steel peg, put a drop of glue on it, and carefully push it down into the hole. It should protrude from the hole by $\frac{1}{8}$". Then, tap it lightly with a hammer to make sure it's in proper contact at the bottom.

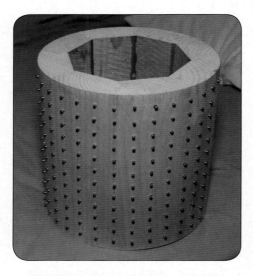

Step 4: Woodwork—Part 2

Hop back on the computer and devise a means to get your shape dimensions onto paper. You can export 2D images from your design software and print them to-scale, or you can just read off dimensions and mark them on the wood with a pencil and a square. When placing things on the wood, remember to keep visible edges away from the biscuits! It helps if your design is on separate cutouts so that you can play with the positioning to maximize wood yield. Remember, the table saw blade will consume about ⅛" of wood, so leave gaps between your pieces.

I'd like to make a safety note. Table saws are horrible, ridiculously dangerous machines. If you are not incredibly afraid of the saw, then *do not* use it. You need a very healthy amount of fear, so that you'll take every precaution when using it, or you'll lose your thumbs. I'm serious.

Once your pieces are cut, there are a few holes to drill. Drill the holes for the shaft that the drum will rotate on and for the sound-port holes on the front piece. Don't drill the holes in the octagonal pieces that will go in the drum yet, since you'll need to properly find the center once they're in place. Now start clamping and gluing. I'll admit, I was on a tight schedule at the time and had to get these parts done in a few hours, so I cheated and used a nail gun. It was a terrible idea, nail guns cause splits in hardwood, so don't do it! Take the time to use glue and clamps properly.

To make the crank handle, cut a 1.5" piece of dowel and a 2" piece of dowel. Cut a piece of leftover oak into a 2" × ½" piece. Drill a ¼" deep hole near one end on one side, and another hole at the other end on the opposite side. Glue one dowel into each hole. The 2" dowel will go inside the machine; 2" may be longer than needed so it can be cut down accordingly.

The way I came up with to glue the end pieces into the wooden drum was like this: First, put wood glue around the outside of the first octagon and lay it flat on the table. Then, put the barrel down on top of it so they fit in together. Make sure they're lined up correctly and wipe off any excess or oozing glue. Wait for it to dry. Then take a center-finding tool and locate the center of this side of the drum. Drill a ¼" to meet your shaft diameter. Now, do the same thing with the second octagon, but this time, to make sure everything is pushed flat and the octagon isn't too far into the barrel, push it with a rod or dowel through the hole in the opposite end. Once the glue is dry, find the center of the second side and drill a second hole. Everything should be perfect!

Cut a 12" length of ¼" solid steel rod for the shaft the drum will rotate on. File the ends so they're smooth.

Step 5: Mechanics

Now we need to start working on the mechanical linkages and crank for the drum movement. Since putting the crank right at drum-level would result in the crank hitting the table, I had to devise some transfer mechanisms to allow me to put it higher up.

I found some plastic gears that meshed correctly with the 8" rubber belt I had for the drum. I glued two of the gears together and glued a long bolt into a hole I drilled through the side of the box. On the end of the box, I drilled a hole and glued a nut into it. This would let me insert a machine screw with a captive armature on it, which held a gear on the end. This would in turn let me tension a transfer belt to prevent slipping of the belts and gears but still make the crank easy to turn.

The result was what you see in the image. The system works pretty well, and I don't think there could be a much easier way to do it without fabricating custom gears.

An important thing to think about is the space you have. There was only about 1" of clearance between the internal wall and the drum, so space was tight.

Step 6: Finishing the Wood

I decided to finish most of the wood early, because I wasn't going to be able to keep working on the project for the next four months, and I didn't want it to get dirty or change shape from water in the air. I just coated it with a few layers of Minwax Polyurethane to make it shiny and bring out the color of the wood a little bit more.

After the polyurethane is dry, squeeze the 8" belt onto the edge of the drum. I cut the belt in half because it was too wide and covered the first row of holes. If it doesn't hold in place by friction alone, you can use finishing nails to tack it in place.

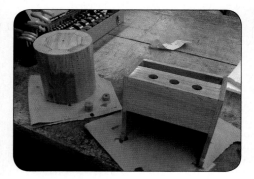

Step 7: The Musical Mechanics

This was a major engineering challenge for quite a while. I had a few designs that were a bust; they were just far too small to be practical. I ended up distilling the ideas into what I think is as simple as could be possible.

The tine, which is a piece of steel from a leaf rake, is sandwiched between two aluminum plates. The tine is kinked at the tip and is roughly the length it needs to be, plus enough length to be held in the plates firmly. This is secured with two small screws that pass through the top plate and into threaded holes in the bottom plate. The bottom plate then sits atop a large aluminum plate with slots machined in it. On the bottom are larger slots with captive nuts in them, held in place against the top of the music box. A screw passes through a hole in the second plate and into one of the nuts so that its position can be controlled by sliding it up and down in the slot. Using this method, the tine length can be tuned to the appropriate note, and then the tine holder can be moved towards the pins on the barrel and lined up for just the right amount of plucking force.

To build the tine holders, I used 1" wide ¼" thick aluminum stock. Since I only had ⅗" of space per tine, I cut the pieces down to 0.59", and then into 0.59" and 1.18" long segments.

The tines can be cut from the rake using a hack saw or angle grinder. Cutting their lengths is a hit-or-miss guessing game, however. Depending on their width, thickness, and composition, their resonating characteristics will change greatly, so I can't give a list of predetermined lengths. You'll have to just cut a few and experiment to find what works for your tines. The tips can be bent with two pairs of pliers.

I used a CNC to cut the aluminum plate. Now, I know that using a CNC is out of the realm of 99% of readers, but I had the resources and it was the best logical way to do the design I had created. If it had to be done using simple tools, I would say sandwich pieces of wood together to form the slots, or use a chisel to carve out the slots for the

nuts and a drill and needle files to do the rest.

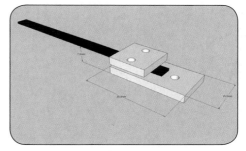

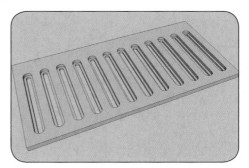

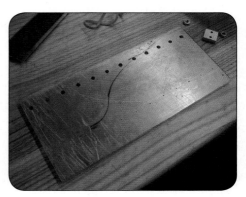

69

The result is a pretty good range of notes that works for lots of little songs, like "Mary Had A Little Lamb," "Hot Cross Buns," and "Pop Goes The Weasel."

To tune, start by arranging all the tines by length, and then place them tightly in the tine holders. Mount all the holders on the aluminum plate, but not near the drum. Tighten them down so they will resonate nicely. Using a piano or a virtual piano (like http://www.virtualpiano.net/), play the note that you want to tune to. Strike the corresponding tine with a plastic mallet. If it is too high, loosen the two screws holding the tine and wiggle the tine out further. If it is too low, push it in further. Once the notes sound right (and you'll know when), you can tighten down the tine as tightly as possible so it can't slip. Then, slide the tine holder up to the drum and put a peg right near it. You want the peg to just barely touch the tine as it comes up and then pluck it. You don't want the tine to bend upwards more than a few millimeters. Too much force could break the tines over time or cause the gears and belts to slip.

Repeat this process until all the tines are tuned. Set up a "test pattern" by placing pegs in diagonal lines across the drum, so it will play the scale when rotated. Test it out! If it sounds good, try out a song or two. You should be able to use music written for a recorder—that should work well on this machine. Chords are possible, but elaborate ones may require more torque to pluck than the crank will allow.

Step 8: Final Assembly and Tuning

Tuning is a pain-staking process that takes an hour or two. The tines can be tuned to lots of different scales, but I selected a simple set of notes from the piano. They are:

- A3
- B3
- C4 (middle C)
- D4
- E4
- F4
- G4
- A4
- B4
- C5
- D5
- E5

never be achieved with wood. If I were to ever try and build something like this again, it would have to be made entirely from metal. Other than that, I don't think the design has any major flaws.

Step 9: Improvements and Considerations

I'll admit, after all the time and effort I put into good design on this project, it didn't turn out as well as I had hoped. Part of the problem is the insane precision required to do this properly, which could

Build an Inexpensive Cigar Box Guitar at Home

By nickdrj
(http://www.instructables.com/id/Build-an-Inexpensive-Cigar-Box-Guitar-at-Home/)

As a birthday present for my brother, I decided to make him a nice cigar box guitar. This is the first one I've ever made so it was a bit of a learning experience.

Before making the guitar, I decided that it should be made from either found or very cheaply obtained materials. Most of the items I used were not originally meant for use in a guitar. I don't think I spent more than $50 for all the parts. It's not a dirt cheap guitar, but it won't hurt the wallet either.

Also, since I don't have any big power tools, I had to be able to make it in my kitchen using the handheld tools I already had (with the exception of the fingerboard, which I had cut for me from a scrap of plywood at a hardware store).

And lastly, I wanted to make this Instructable because I wanted to share everything I learned, plus to give back for all the helpful guides I used for this project. This project has a lot of steps, so I tried to divide it up in to logical sections.

Tools
- Dremmel (best tool ever)
- Different sandpapers
- Couple of different files
- Coping saw
- Drill
- A lot of clamps
- Hot glue
- Epoxy

Step 1: The Body

The cigar box! I found this nice box at a cigar shop that sells them for $2. (I'm paying for garbage!) It's important to find a box you really like; it will make your guitar stand out! I liked this one because it had rounded sides, which made it really uncommon.

Since the neck will be glued to the top of the box lid, I first made a cut where the neck will go through. I cut it down with a saw and then filed it down. Next I wanted two circular sound holes on either side of the guitar; this way, I can run the neck all the way down the body. I also wanted to make the rims of the sound holes be metal. So I found a nice chrome metal pipe at Home Depot that had nice rims at the end. I cut those off with my coping saw.

I also want the option of this guitar being played electrically, so I will install a piezo pickup in a later step. But I have to make a hole for the mono jack. Since the jack is pretty short, I had to grind down the inside of the box where the jack will be installed. Check the pictures for what I mean.

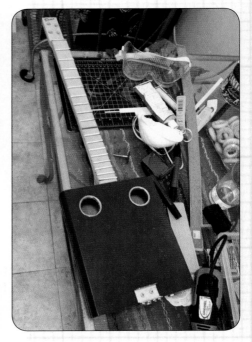

Step 2: The Neck

The neck basically will take up 90 percent of your time. I wanted it to be nice and round at the back, have a base where it connects to the body (much like an acoustic), and be fretted. For the structure, I wanted to keep it simple and run the neck along the whole body, eventually gluing it to the top of the cigar box.

First things first: I cut the neck to the desired length. I didn't use any conventional length, I just picked it intuitively, whatever felt right. Then I cut the hole in the box where the neck will be glued. This gives me an idea where to add the base.

After cutting the neck, I started to work on the heel at the bottom of the neck. I cut out two pieces of wood about 4" long from the remaining neck wood. I glued them together using Titebond wood glue. Using a clamp, I pressed them together and let it dry for thirty minutes. Then I glued the two pieces onto the main neck board.

Next, I cut the glued heel to the desired profile with my coping saw. Finally, I shaped it using a file.

Step 3: The Head

I wanted the head of the guitar to be slightly recessed so that the strings get more tension. First, I glued another piece of wood to the back of the head. I cut it from the same wood as the neck, and then cut it in half, so that it was about ¼" thick. Then I grinded it down with a file to make it nice and curved. Next I cut ¼" off the front of the head. Then I filed everything down to make it as smooth as I could get it. After that, I did my best to guess where to put the holes for the tuner. I then drilled them. I don't have power tools so it got a little splintery around the edges. No big deal though, it gets covered up by the tuners. Lastly, I put in a decal at the top. I put my brother's name. I used a technique where I printed it in reverse on acetate then glued it on with photo mount. Then later, when I apply the finish, it gets sealed. Since the neck and head is complete, I smoothed out the back with a file to make it nice and round.

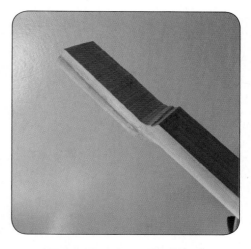

strings using the Dremel. Lastly, I drilled a couple of holes at the bottom and screwed it into the body of the guitar.

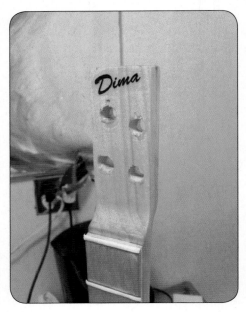

Step 4: The Bridge

The bridge I made in two parts. First, to hold the strings in place, I used a heavy duty picture hanger I got at Home Depot (sawing off the peg that is used for hanging). I used a large screw to keep it in place. The screw went through the cigar box and into the piece of wood for the neck, making it a pretty solid fit. Then, in the trash I found a handle that was attached to a drawer that had been thrown away. This turned out to be perfect for the saddle—it just needed some shaping. I chopped off the sides and cut it down a bit so the action wasn't so high. Then I added notches for the

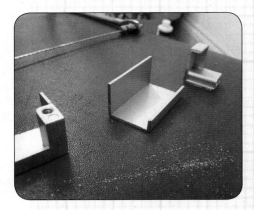

hanger. I cut up the wire using big wire cutters (later a Dremel—so much easier). Make sure to cut them a little long—you will grind them down to shape. I then glued on the very top fret using epoxy.

At this point, I measured very accurately the distance from the top fret to the bridge. This is very important as it will determine the spacing of the fret. Then I went to stewmac.com. They have a very good fret calculator. I inserted the length of the scale and how many frets I wanted. Using the measurements stewmac.com provided, I penciled them all in one by one. Remember to always measure from the top fret; don't measure fret to fret, because it is easier to make a mistake and screw up the notes. After penciling them in, I used a coping saw to saw little gutters for the frets. You may need to go into them using a file as well.

When done, you can glue the frets into place using epoxy. Use a piece of wood and clamps to hold the frets in place while the glue dries. Once they are glued solidly, cut the edges off using a Dremel with a cutting attachment. Wear eye protection—sparks will fly.

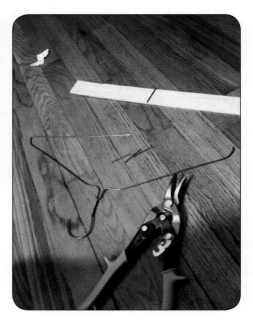

Step 5: Fretting

I got a piece of plywood scrap cut to size at a hardware store; it's basically the thickness of the neck. I cut it lengthwise and glued it on to the neck. Keeping with the goal of using found/cheap materials, I decided to use wire cut from a common

Step 6: Fret Dots

I only decided to add fret marks on the side of the neck. To do this, I basically drilled holes on the 3rd, 5th, 7th, 9th, and 12th frets (double holes for 12). Then, I hammered tiny nails into the holes, sawed them off with my Dremel, and filed them down. Easy!

Step 7: Peizo Pickup

The Piezo pickup is a really easy way to get any acoustic guitar to play electrically. The one thing I'd recommend is getting one that is easy to disassemble, so you can get the metal plate that acts as the mic out. The one I got from RadioShack was sealed shut, and I had to grind up the plastic to get to the piezo element inside. After removing it, I soldered two wires to the yellow ones that came with the piezo element. Then I coiled them together.

Inside the box, I added loop screws to run the wire and soldered it to the mono jack I installed earlier. I installed the piezo element using a bit of hot glue from a glue gun to raise it above the wood.

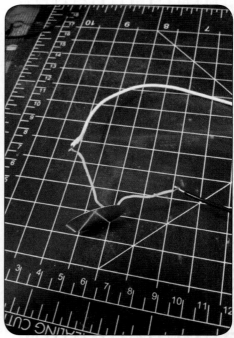

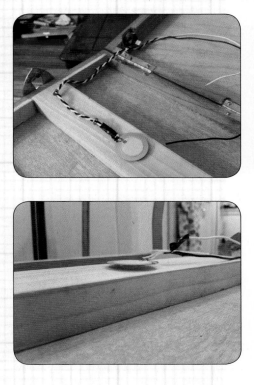

Step 8: Applying the Finish

Applying the finish to the neck is pretty straightforward. I used a clear lacquer for the job. I covered the frets up with some masking tape, so that they wouldn't get all sticky. I know I'm probably doing this backwards, but it is what it is . . . I applied a coat and waited about an hour. Once it was dry, I used a fine sandpaper to smooth it out. Then, I repeated a couple of more times. And that's it.

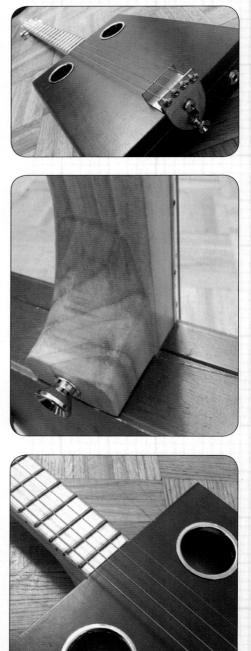

Step 9: Finished!

And here is the finished guitar. It wasn't too difficult to make, just a bit time consuming. It was a great learning experience. I hope to improve on it in the next one. And I hope it helps anyone else making these fun DIY instruments.

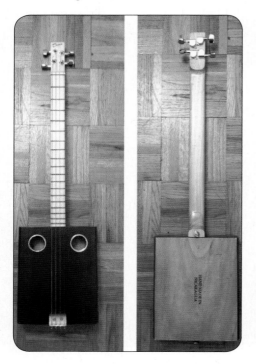

Scroll-Sawed Wooden Bowls

By Jake Elmer (LMO)
(http://www.instructables.com/
id/Scroll-Sawed-Wooden-Bowls/)

I was disappointed recently to find that there are no Instructables on making wooden bowls with a scroll saw, even though there are lots of books published on the subject. So I've decided to fill the gap.

All you'll need is a scroll saw and a few other tools to get started. I like this project because it minimizes the amount of wasted wood (unlike bowls made with a lathe), and the bowls produced have very interesting designs. It's also surprisingly easy, as long as you have the patience to sand it to perfection.

Step 1: Tools and Materials

Tools
- Scroll saw (mandatory)
- Table saw
- Miter saw
- Planer
- Jointer
- Drill press with adjustable stage (for different angles)
- Belt/disc sander
- Digital caliper/straight edge

Materials
- Wood glue
- Scroll saw blades (they will break often)
- Pen/pencil
- Clamps, clamps, and more clamps
- Sandpaper and sandpaper belts for sanders
- Varnish (and/or stain, depending on what you want to do)
- At least 1' of wood, can be pieces of various woods

Note: If you plan on putting food in the bowl, you should avoid using exotic hardwoods. Many of those woods contain toxic chemicals, which can contaminate food and possibly harm you. However, most domestic hardwoods are fine for use with food.

Step 2: Wood and Laminates

The first step is to prepare the blank from which you will cut the bowl pieces. I recommend making the blank at least 12" × 12". It can be a solid piece of wood or a laminate of several different types of wood. If you use more pieces with contrasting colors, it makes the final design on the bowl much more impressive. I used a parallel laminate of three types of wood for this project, but you can do far more just by changing the thickness of the strips or gluing them together at different angles.

Here are the general steps for making a good laminate:

1. Cut the desired strips to the desired width with a table saw.
2. Use a miter saw to cut the strips to the desired length.
3. Use a jointer to smooth and level the sides of the strips.
4. Fit the pieces together to make sure there are no gaps.

Step 3: Gluing the Laminate

Special care must be taken while gluing the strips of the laminate together to avoid warping. Choose a flat surface that you can use clamps with and clean it. Look ahead to Step 7 before gluing. Apply a good amount of glue to each piece and join them together. Do not glue the middle two pieces together if you want to avoid drilling entry holes, as mentioned in Step 7. Carefully wipe up excess glue. Use long clamps to squeeze the pieces together. Use more clamps to keep the laminate flat on the table/surface. Wipe up any more excess glue. Let the glue dry for about twenty-four hours at or above 55°F.

Step 4: Finishing the Laminate

I highly recommend using a planer to smooth the laminate and to get rid of any warping that may have occurred during gluing. Once you have smooth surfaces on both sides of the laminate, measure its thickness at multiple points to make sure the piece is even.

Step 5: Choosing Bowl Dimensions

The simplest way to make a bowl is to cut the rings at a 45° angle. That way, the rings are as far apart as the laminate is thick. I recommend the diameter of the inner circle be at least 3".

If you want to try different dimensions to make unique bowls, grab a calculator or open up Excel and follow the steps below:

1. Choose a diameter for the inner circle (should be 3–4"): D, cell A2
2. Measure the maximum length/ diameter of the laminate: L, cell B2
3. Measure the thickness of the laminate: T, cell C2
4. Choose an angle to cut: (theta), cell D2
5. Calculate width of each ring: X, cell E2
6. Cut and paste this formula into cell E2: =TAN(RADIANS(D2))*C2
7. Calculate the number of rings (round down): N, cell F2
8. Cut and paste this formula into cell F2: =FLOOR((B2-A2)/(2*E2),1)
9. Calculate the final height of the bowl: H, cell G2
10. Cut and paste this formula into cell G2: =(F2+1)*C2
11. Play around with the cut angle (theta) until you are happy with the final height of the bowl.

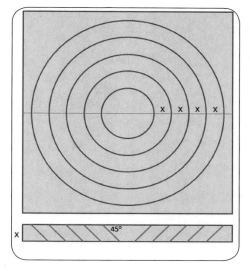

Step 6: Trace the Circles

Once you have calculated the width of each ring (X from last step), you will need to trace the rings onto the bowl, like so:

1. Find the center of the blank and mark it with an X.

	A	B	C	D	E	F	G
1	D	L	T	theta	X	N	H
2	3	12	0.5	45	0.5	9	5
3	inches	inches	inches	degrees	inches	#	inches

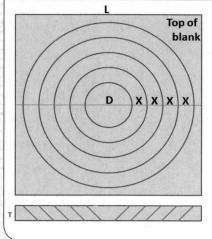

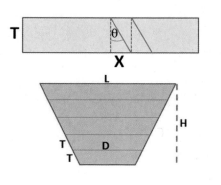

2. Take a stiff piece of card stock (ex: cover of a notebook or holiday card) and cut a 1" wide by 6–12" long strip.
3. On one end of the strip, make a tiny hole with the point of a knife.
4. Draw a straight line from that hole across the length of the strip.
5. Make another hole about "D/2" inches along that line from the first hole.
6. Make more holes, each "X" inches apart, until you've reached the maximum radius of your bowl.
7. Pin the strip down to the blank with a pointy object and carefully trace concentric circles by rotating the strip around the centerpoint on the blank (see below).

angle that will be used to allow you to start cutting. If you have a good drill press and a strong thin bit, you can use this method.

However, I don't have a good drill press, so I can't make consistent entry holes. Therefore, I came up with a way to avoid having to drill them. I simply make the laminate in even halves and cut semi-circles, which are later glued together to give full circles. That way, I don't have to worry about the accuracy of entry holes or putting on/taking off my scroll saw blade. See the second picture below to see exactly what I'm talking about.

Step 7: Optional: Drilling Entry Holes

Most traditional wood bowls start with a solid piece of wood. To start cutting the rings, entry holes must be drilled with the scroll saw at the same

Step 8: Cutting the Rings

Now it is time to warm up that scroll saw! The method here is pretty self explanatory—just cut the rings out and take your time. Here are some extra pointers:

- Make sure the stage on the scroll saw is adjusted to the proper angle. Cut a test piece and measure the angle, if necessary.
- Go slowly, but never stop moving forward. If you stop or go back, you will remove more wood and scar the bowl.
- Maintain lots of pressure on the piece for a clean, consistent, and quick cut.

Step 9: Glue

Before you do any gluing, mark the pieces so you can glue them together exactly as they were cut. If you forget to do this, some of the bands may not match up properly. If you avoided drilling entry holes, the first thing to do now is to glue the half circles together to make full circles. Use plenty of glue and clamp them down on a flat surface until dry.

Once you have the rings glued, glue them together, one at a time. Make sure that the bands on the outside of the bowl line up as nicely as possible. If you have a spindle sander, don't glue the bottom piece onto the bowl just yet. Leaving the bottom of the bowl open will allow you to easily sand the inside of the bowl using a spindle sander. If you don't have a spindle sander, go ahead and glue the bottom piece.

Put the glued bowl onto a flat surface and compress it with something heavy. Some people use "bowl presses" (Google it), but I just use my old textbooks. Compress the bowl for at least a few hours or until the glue has dried overnight.

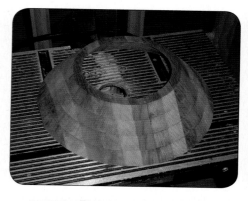

Step 10: Sanding

No matter how good your cuts were, there's a lot of sanding to be done! I prefer a belt sander for this step. I smooth out the outside and inside of the bowl with about 50-grit sand paper, then move up to 120-grit to make it even smoother for finishing. Examine the bowl carefully, rubbing your fingers across the joints to make sure they are as smooth as possible.

I also like to round off the edge of the bowl with my disc sander. Just take your time and evenly sand the edge of the bowl. Be careful not to lose control—disc sanders can quickly gouge your bowl.

Finally, I like to thoroughly sand the inside and outside of the bowl with 120-grit sandpaper to get any small spots the belt sander may have missed.

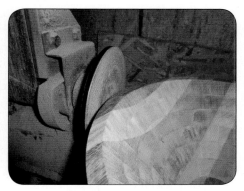

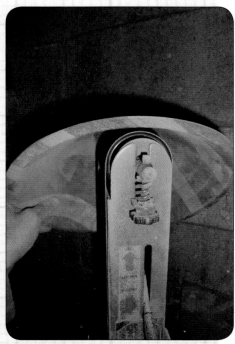

Step 11: Finishing Touches

Once the bowl is smooth, wipe it down with a wet cloth to remove any dust particles. Let it dry, then apply a one to three coats of varnish. Smooth out/sand with a high grit sandpaper as necessary.

How to Make a Steel Vase

By Cameron Bell (cammers)
(http://www.instructables.com/
id/How-to-Make-a-Steel-Vase-
Step-by-Step/)

I really enjoy turning scrap steel into objects that some people might find beautiful. The first picture shows a few of my pieces. I normally give my work away to friends or trade it for something completely different that, for example, a friend has created.

I have had some success using flat steel plate to make three-dimensional objects. In this Instructable, I will attempt to share the process so others might enjoy the experience, too. I don't intend to provide a pattern so you can make an identical object—I'm sure you will want something unique. I will simply outline the steps I took so you can see how easy it is.

Step 1: Inspiration and Planning

Inspiration can come from anywhere. Sometimes I can spend hours staring at image searches on the web. Sometimes I can walk into my workshop and just start making. This time I had a pair of old Chinese jars that I stole proportions from.

Working with flat steel, it helps to choose a design that can be broken down into a series of flat planes. In this case, I measured my old jars and drew a simple 3D sketch in AutoCAD. It looked okay, so I then drew all the faces on the one plane, trying to lay them out to minimize the required cutting. There were only three shapes: the hexagon base and two trapezoids making up the tapered sides and the shoulders.

Of course it's just as good to use a pen, a ruler, or even trace the outline of the object.

Since I could only print in A4, I decided to only print those three shapes—joined as they would be when making up the base and one side of the pot. I cut out the print with scissors and used that for my template.

Step 2: Marking Out

First find some steel. I prefer to work with free stuff that has been discarded. Chequer plate has a great texture. So does old rusty steel after it has been cleaned up a bit. In my example, I chose a sheet of steel about 1.5mm thick. In a previous life, it had been used as a pallet to mix concrete on, so it took a lot of work to get it clean.

Work out the most efficient way of laying out the shapes needed and then, using your template, mark them out with chalk or soap stone.

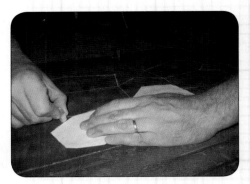

Step 3: Cut Out

I use a thin cutting disc on my angle grinder. I see a lot of very high-tech cutting machines on Instructables these days, but sadly I don't have one. Simply cut out the outline and lightly score any line that will need to be folded.

Step 4: Start Bending and Welding and Grinding and More Grinding

Using a vise, gloved hands, pliers, hammer, or whatever you can get hold of, gradually bend each fold one at a time until the sides are close enough to their final position for tacking.

I used a hammer to get joints tight enough to weld. When a joint is closed, tack it and move to the next. Close the joint and tack. And so on until the sides are all welded. Then bend the shoulders down and weld.

I left some steel at the tops of each shoulder piece in order to make a rim. I bent the rim pieces out as I formed the shoulders. These took some hammering to get them right for welding. (I'm actually not convinced the rim is necessary. I might just chop it off.)

If you are as rough a welder as me, you will now need to do a lot of grinding to make the thing look a bit neat. At this point, I also trimmed the rim.

Step 5: Conclusion

There are many different ways to do a job like this. I have given a very brief and deliberately vague outline of the method I chose, hoping that this will be enough to inspire someone to get started on their own path.

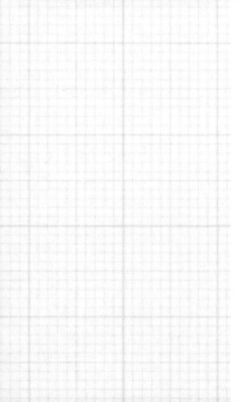

How To Make a Metal Rose

By Michael Downard and Ryan Downard (Downard Works)

(http://www.instructables.com/id/How-to-Make-a-Metal-Rose/)

The first thing you want to do when making a metal rose is make sure you have everything you will need to complete the project.

Materials
- Scrap or non-scrap metal
- A metal rod

Tools
- Angle grinder with cutting and grinding wheels
- Pliers (needle-nose preferably)
- Bench vice
- Arc welder with welding rods
- Propane torch with propane
- Drill press and drill bits
- A marking tool (sharpie, chalk, wax pencil, etc.)
- A ruler
- Safety gear
- Plasma cutter (optional)

Disclaimer: Any one who is injured in the process of making this project is responsible for his or her own injury. We are in no way responsible for any injury that may occur while building this. Proceed at your own risk.

Step 1: Cutting Out the Circles

You will need to cut out three circles from your scrap metal. First, you need to mark the circles on the scrap metal, using a stencil to trace your circles—either a paint can or a roll of tape or anything with a flat edge that is round. After you have your circles drawn, you then proceed to cut them out. Using either a plasma torch or an angle grinder, cut out the circles as round as you can. You will end up with three similar disks. Don't worry about cleaning up the edges; that will come later.

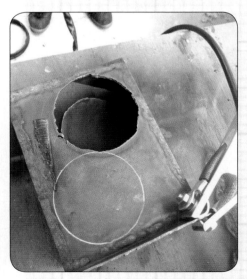

Step 2: Measuring and Cutting the Petals

For this step, you will need your ruler and angle grinder (or plasma torch). First you must find five points on the perimeter of the disk that are evenly spaced. You can do this several ways. Either take measurements and mark your points, or you could draw a star with the points touching the edge of the disk until it looks right. Either way you choose to do it, you will end up with five marks on the edge of the disk. Now you will draw them all to the middle of the circle until they meet at one point. This means it's time for cutting. When you're cutting the petals into the disk, be sure not to cut all the way down the line—there needs to be enough room for the hole that will be drilled though it.

Step 3: Clean Up the Edges

Now that we have the petals cut in, it's time to clean up the edges of the disk and to finish shaping the petals. For this you will need your angle grinder with the grinding and cutting disk. Be sure that the cuts are straight and all the way though the petals. Run the grinder over the surface of the petal disk repeatedly until it is smooth or shiny. Once the disk is smooth, round the sharp corners of the petals. This will make it safer and give it a more realistic petal look. Don't rush yourself on this step. How well you smooth the petals and round the corners will determine the look of the final product.

way past the previous cut. Remember to check that each weld is a good one before continuing onto the next one.

Step 4: Drilling and Welding

Now we will begin the process of attaching the petals to the stem. For this you will need a drill press and an arc welder. First, make sure the place is marked where you need to drill the hole. When drilling the hole, be sure to not use your hand to hold it. Use pliers or a vice or something. If it starts spinning on the drill bit, it will slice your hand up. Also be sure to drill a small hole to start the process. Then work your way up in drill bit sizes until you have the size hole you want.

Once all three holes are drilled, take it to the welder. You will weld them from the top of the petals, so the next set of petals will sit on the previous weld. This is all the spacing that you will need for it to look good. Be sure to weld the petals so the cuts don't line up, or else it wont look like a rose when it's finished. A good rule of thumb is to rotate the next disk so the cuts are one third of the

Step 5: Heating and Shaping

Now it's time for the final step. For this you will need a propane torch and pliers. Heat the petals so that they are red hot. Be sure not to burn yourself on them; never reach over the top of them. They must be bent in a pattern or else they wont look right. One side of the petal should lie on the inside of another while the other half of the petal is covering the one next to it. Keep the top petals tight so the other petals can be folded up with enough room. It will take several heatings to bend all the petals. Once you're done folding the petals up, get creative with them. Organic things are never symmetrical. After you're happy with your new rose, clean out the flakes of metal from the inside and quench the metal by spraying it with the water hose. The rest is up to you. You can paint it or leave it as is. You could even make a vine of them. Turn them into art. Like this gate for instance.

Duct Tape Projects

- -

High-Quality Tote Bag

By Chris O'Donnell
(CODO69)

(http://www.instructables.com/
id/High-Quality-Duct-Tape-
Tote-Bag/)

This is my newest creation, a 15" × 15" × 4" woven duct tape tote/purse. It's super sturdy and quite impressive!

Step 1: Items Needed

- Approximately 120 yd of duct tape (I used three different colors with two rolls being 60 yd each of black)
- A scissors
- A razor blade
- Ruler/tape measure
- Cardboard
- Pen/pencil/marker
- 550 cord/paracord (parachute cord)
- (Magnets optional)

Step 2: Tape Sheets

1. Using the color tape that you have the most of (mine was black), cut a strip of tape 15.5". Lay the first one down glue side up. Carefully line up the second strip over the first (glue side to glue side) overlapping the widths half way. Fold over the second half of the exposed glue-side-up strip to make a clean edge.

2. Flip the combined strips over, leaving glue side up. Lay the next layer down, overlapping tape layers about 0.25" to 0.5".

3. Repeat step 2 until the sheet of tape is 15" exactly.

   Note: Using a ruler (mine was 16" long), I measured a straight line on the table to align my final strip of tape so it would be straight and measured the sheet so it would line up with the line I drew exactly 15" away.

4. Using your ruler and the razor, cut a straight edge on the uneven edges, leaving a clean line. Repeat on the other side and measure to make sure it's 15" wide. You should now have a solid sheet of duct tape that is exactly 15" × 15".

   Note: Cut as close to the first uneven edge as possible, without leaving a jagged edge of tape. This should leave enough room on the other side to play with to make a clean cut.

5. Repeat steps 1–4 again leaving you with two 15" × 15" sheets.

6. Repeat steps 1–4 again, but this time make two sheets that are 4" × 15".

   Note: Set these sheets aside for later use.

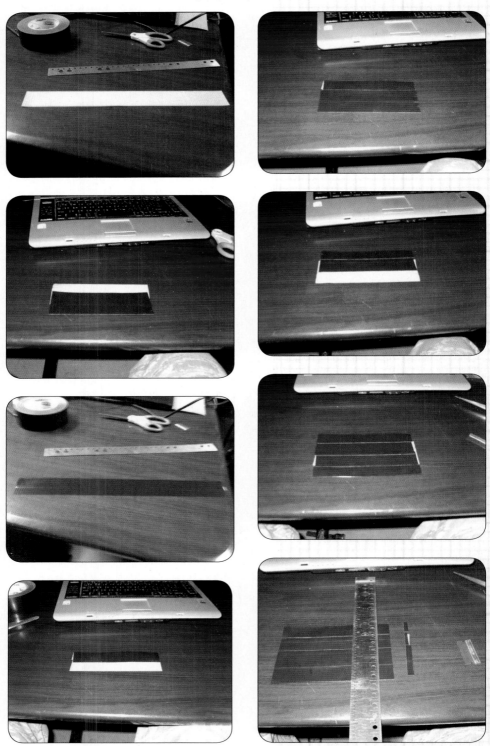

(I have six 15.25" strips of black, twelve 15.25" strips of orange, and thirty 15.25" strips of white for this pattern.)

Note: The strips are all slightly longer than they need to be to accommodate the shortening of the strips through the weaving process to come.

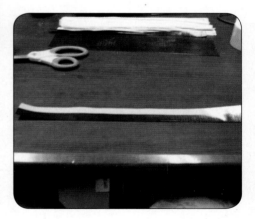

Step 3: Woven Strips

The following steps will need to be repeated a *lot*! You've been warned.

1. Your will need to cut a strip of tape that is 38".
2. Fold the tape lengthwise into approximate thirds (about 5/8" folded over).
3. Fold the tape over again, making one strip.
4. Repeat steps 1–3 until you have 20 strips total of the 38" strips—yes, 20 total.
5. Repeat steps 1–3 again, making two strips totaling 5 ft (60") long. These will be your handles for the bag.
6. Depending on the pattern you have planned on, you'll need to repeat steps 1–3 again until you have 48 strips total, all 15.25" long.

Step 4: Purse Bottom

First, get your cardboard; the stiffer the better!

1. Cut out two rectangles measuring 15" × 4", with the corrugation running lengthwise.
2. Cut out a rectangle measuring 15" × 4", with the corrugation running widthwise.
3. Stack the layers together so the corrugation is alternating, with the widthwise corrugation in the middle.
4. Cover the entire stack in tape, making a solid plank. Make sure to cover all the edges.

Step 5: Assembly of the Inner Bag

For my design, I covered the top of the cardboard plank in white to make it easy to see into the bottom of the bag. That will come later.

Grab the two 15" × 15" sheets and the two 15" × 4" sheets.

1. We'll work with the 4" wide sheet first. With the strips of the sheets running vertically (the cut edges on top and bottom), align the bottom edge to the bottom edge of the plank. Using a 4" strip of tape, lay it over the bottom edge of the sheet half way and fold the rest over the underside of the plank.
2. With the sheet standing up (or hanging down depending how you look at it) apply another 4" strip to the inside edge.

3. Repeat steps 1 and 2 for the remaining three sides. (This is when I applied the white tape to the plank.)

Note: Now comes a little bit of a tricky part. A second pair of helping hands may be beneficial.

4. Using a 15" strip of tape, tape up the seam of the two sheets on the outer edge. Keep the edges tightly together.
5. Using a 15" strip of tape, tape up the seam of the two sheets on the inner edge. Get the tape as far into the crease as you can (bend it flat if you can). You should notice about 0.5" of tape overhanging the top of the sheet. Trim it off flush with the sheet.
6. Repeat steps 4 and 5 with the other three seams. Keep in mind that the closer you get to the final seam, the harder it will be to get the inside seam flat. (This is where an extra set of hands comes in handy to help apply the tape).

Note: Once the bag is finished, set it aside for later.

Step 6: Assembly of the Woven Sheet

Prepare to spend a lot of time taping and weaving!

Grab yourself a 15.5" strip and a 36" strip. Throughout the rest of this stage and pretty much the rest of the Instructable, you will be using literally 1,000+ pieces of tape that are about 1" × 0.5"! (Let's call these small pieces of tape tacks.)

Note: It is important that you make sure, from here on out, all the strips of tape have the exposed folded edge all facing the same side! This will make a cleaner looking finished product. Also, I will be describing in generality for the pattern. But if you care to repeat it, possibly with different colors, the pattern will go (lengthwise from top to bottom) six white, three orange, six white, three orange, three white, six black, three white, three orange, six white, three orange, six white.

1. At the end of the 36" strip, tape half of the tack to it. Align the long strip perpendicular to the 15.25" strip. Fold the other half of the tack underneath the 15.25" strip.
2. Repeat step 1 directly next to the first 36" strip, making sure that the long strips are touching edge to edge. But this time put the long strip under the 15.25" strip and fold the tack over instead of under.
3. Repeat steps 1 and 2 until you have the first seven columns of 36" strips taped.
4. For the eighth column of long strips, grab one of the two 60" long strips. Measure 17.25" from the tape end down on the seventh column strip and note where the mark is. This is where the end of the 60" strip should start. Following the over-under pattern, tack the eighth column to the 15.25" strip and gently lay the excess strip to the side.

5. Using the 36" strips again, repeat steps 1 and 2 again until you have six more columns applied.

6. For the 15th column, grab the other end of the 60" strip and measure out 17.25" like you did in step 4. Tack the handle in place (still using the over-under weaving pattern).

Note: Make sure the strip isn't twisted up and that the folded exposed edge of the strip curves around so that it's the underside of the strap.

7. Using the 36" strips again, repeat steps 1 and 2 again until you have seven more columns applied. This should bring you to the end of the 15.25" strip. Tack the ends down, and, if a slight bit of strip overhangs past the last 36" strip, trim it off (it's why we made it a touch longer).

8. Grab your next 15.25" strip, and as stated . . . start weaving, over and under opposite to the previous row. I find it easier to tuck the row under one column at a time.

Note: Make sure you pull the rows together as tight as you can without bending or creasing the two of them *while simultaneously* keeping the columns straight and as tight together as you can without bending or creasing them. A nice tight weave!

9. Repeat step 8 for the next eight rows, making nine in total.

10. Set it aside for a bit. Now we're going to get a little more creative!

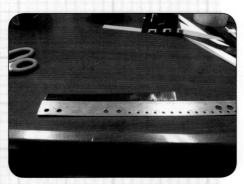

Step 7: Assembly of the Woven Pockets

We'll be weaving pockets in the same manner as the outer woven sheet.

1. We need to cut eight strips at 8.75". (For my design, these are the six white and two orange horizontal strips.)
2. Next we need to cut ten strips at 7" (the black vertical strips).
3. Fold the strips into thirds again like back in step 3 (the 36", 60", and 15.25" strips).
4. Grab your first horizontal strip (orange). Fold it in half and note where the center mark is. In the over-under styling of the previous step, tack the ten vertical strips (black) to the first horizontal strip.

   Note: Keep in mind that you need to keep the strips perpendicular to each other.
5. Grab the next horizontal 8.75" strip. Keeping the ends lined up, weave the strips together, tacking the new row to the previous row as in Step 6: Assembly of the Woven Sheet.
6. Repeat step 5 until all eight rows are woven together.
7. Cut a strip of tape to go edge to edge from the first to last vertical strip. Lay the edge of the tape directly over the first row, sealing the woven strips together. Fold the rest of the tape over to the back side. Press firmly.
8. With the finished pocket, flip the whole thing over. Cut strips long enough to go edge to edge from the first to last vertical strips.
9. Now, overlay these cut strips over the back of the pocket, covering all the tacks. Each layer of these strips will overlap about 0.5". This will give it a clean and finished look, especially when you open the pocket.

   Set this woven pocket to the side for a few minutes; we'll get back to it shortly.

Next, we'll be assembling two side pockets that we'll be attaching later.

10. You'll need to cut strips out at the following lengths: six horizontal strips 6" long and seven vertical strips 5" long.

11. Repeat step 3 for all the strips you just cut.

12. This time when you fold the first row in half, note where the center mark is. This is where the center of the seven vertical strips will be placed for proper spacing.

13. Repeat steps 5–9 until you have finished the side pocket.

14. Trim all the loose ends flush and make them the length of one vertical row past the first and last vertical row.

15. Repeat steps 10–14 again to make a second pocket.

Set these two smaller pockets aside for now.

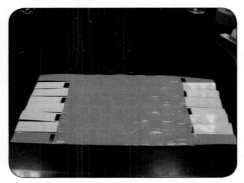

Step 8: Assembly of Woven Sheet Continued

Alright now comes the fun part—attaching the front pocket to the woven sheet.

Now that the front pocket is pre-made and we have our woven sheet with the first nine rows woven, it's time to combine the two into one.

1. Take your pocket and lay it over the woven sheet. In my pattern, you'll notice the pocket will span from the last orange strip across the six white strips and end on the first orange strip of the three in the pattern. You'll also notice that the spacing of the handles is eight columns from handle strip to handle strip, while the pocket you made spans ten columns.

2. You'll need four strips measuring 5/8" × 2", plus one tack strip per row for all the rows of the pocket to adhere it.

3. With your pocket lying over the woven sheet, locate where the last column is and move one more to the right. You'll see where the loose end of the first row lays over the last row of the sheet. Tuck the 2" long strip behind the last row of the sheet, making sure the edge of the strip is flush with the bottom edge of the row. This will help conceal any unsightly seam lines. Wrap the 2" strip over the top of the pocket's first-row loose end and tuck

it under the back side of the last row of the sheet.

4. Weave the rest of this loose end under the next column and over the following one. Repeat the tucking of the 2" strip behind the back row, over the pocket row, and underneath the back row again. There should be just enough loose end left that you can lay it under the following column. It'll be covered when you continue the weaving process.

5. Repeat steps 3 and 4 for the left side of the pocket on the first row. The only difference is with the weave: when you weave the loose end under the third column, snip off any excess and just tack the loose end under the column.

Note: Any time the loose ends go over a column when weaving, you'll use the 2" strip to hold it, and any time it ends under the column, you just need to use a tack.

Now that the top row of the pocket is woven into the sheet, we need to continue not only the pockets but the rest of the sheet.

6. Flip the sheet with the now-attached pocket upside down. Grab your next 15.25" strip and weave/tack it into place on the woven sheet as you did for the first nine rows. (In my pattern, the next color was white, which matches the next row of the pocket). Once finished, flip the entire thing over again.

7. Repeat steps 3–5 with the second row of the pocket. Keep in mind to follow the pattern of the weave. It will be opposite of the previous row. Use the three 5/8" × 2" strips and the one tack on this second row to adhere this row of the pocket.

8. Continue to do steps 6 and 7 for the rest of rows of the pocket.

9. With the pocket now fully attached/woven in, we can continue with the simpler process of weaving just the sheet. Continue your pattern in guidance with steps from Step 6: Assembly of the Woven Sheet.

10. When you finally reach the halfway mark, you'll see you have come to the end of the handle strips. Take the second 60" strip and tape the ends of the strips to one another. Continue the weaving process.

11. With all of the rows finally finished, you should have some loose ends hanging out at the ends of the 36" strips. Trim these ends flush with the final row of the sheet and tack all of the ends to the final row.

Now that all of the loose ends are trimmed and tacked in place, it's time to finish off the sheet.

12. Like when making the pockets, we're going to seal up the backside. You'll need to cut strips 15" long and line the back of the sheet, covering all the tack strips. Overlay each strip about 0.5".

13. Just like the top edges of the pockets, we need to lay tape the exact length and width of the sheet over the outer rows and columns, and fold it over to the back side. Now you have a finished woven sheet with all edges sealed up. For the edges with the handles, you'll need to make a few cuts so you can wrap the tape around the handle. I cut a slit at the very base of the handle (in the tape to be folded over) matching the width of the handle. Then, on the inner edge of the handle, I cut at 90 degrees from the slit I had just made to the edge of the tape to be wrapped over. This will allow the tape to wrap over and around the handle and will seal everything up nicely.

To strengthen the handle straps, I went with 10 ft of 550 cord/paracord/parachute cord. The sheath has a breaking point of about 305 lbs. I fully understand that this may seem like a slight overkill for the weight ratio, but it's easily flattened and certainly strong enough. The inner strands hold about 35 pounds a strand, but I didn't want the thin strands potentially cutting their way through the tape of the straps over time.

14. Remove all the inner strands from the outer sheath.

15. Laying the sheath approximately 1/4 of the way down the length of the woven sheet (in line with the handle straps), tape the sheath to the back edge of the woven sheet.

    This next step is a little troublesome.

16. Cut a strip of tape about 25" long. Lining up the end of the tape to the edge of the sheet, tape the strip along the entire length of the handle. Center the strap in the middle of the tape strip even while it curves around the handle.

    Note: Be careful not to let the tape fold in on itself and get stuck to anything else.

17. Lay the sheath on the underside of the handle strap, and carefully fold over one edge of the tape over the sheath and the other side. *Press firmly* on the seam you just created.

18. Route the sheath across the length of the woven sheet and repeat steps 16 and 17 again.

19. You'll have several inches of rope overlapping each other. Tape the rope down and press firmly all along the seams.

    For the purpose of my pattern, I later added a 5/8" × ~25" strip of orange to the underside of the handle straps. It gave it accent coloring, and it covered up and helped seal the seams of tape holding in the rope.

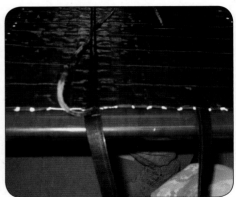

Step 9: Assembly of the Side Pockets

Now we will attach the side pockets to the inner bag.

The first thing you may notice is that the side pockets are just a tad wider than the width of the 4" inner bag we made back in Step 1: Assembly of the Inner Bag. This is fine; if we made it just 4", the pocket would be too tight to use it for anything useful. This will give it a slight bowing out. The front pocket didn't need because since the sidewall is flexible.

Before I got started with this step, I covered both 4" wide side walls of the bag in orange.

1. Grab the two side pockets you created earlier and the inner bag.
2. Cut two strips of tape four to 4.5" long. Align one strip to each side of the pocket. It should completely cover the loose ends (the black strips, not the orange ones.)
3. Align the one edge of the outer vertical strip to the edge of the bag. (Make sure the edge of the bottom of the last horizontal row is flush with the bottom edge of the bag.) Tape the pocket to the back with the already attached to the pocket.

4. Wrap the pocket around to the other edge of the 4" wall and tape it down in the same manner.
5. Cut yourself seven strips of 0.5" × 2" tape. Starting with the center vertical row loose end, tack the loose end down to the underside of the bag. Do so with the other loose ends, working from the center outwards.

Note: To make it look better, as I moved outwards taping the loose ends down, I taped them on an increasing angle to help keep the bowing shape of the pocket.
6. To help seal it all in place, cut a strip of tape about 13" long and wrap it from one sidewall, down underneath (over the 2" long tacks), and back up the other side wall. Press firmly.
7. Repeat steps 2–6 for the pocket on the other side of the bag.

Step 10: Finalizing Assembly

As a last minute idea, I decided to put some magnets in this tote bag. Now, since this is pretty thick with layers of duct tape, I needed something pretty strong. Being resourceful, I dismantled a broken portable hard drive and stripped it of the two rare earth magnets that were inside—just the perfect strength and size for what I needed. I simply taped them on the outside of the inner bag with a square of tape. And they won't be visible when the woven sheet is fixed to the inner bag.

Depending on how well and straight you wove the outer sheet will affect how easy it will be to put the two pieces together. I found it easier to lay the top edge of the inner bag to the top edge of the woven sheet.

1. Just like back in Step 8: Assembly of the Woven Sheet Continued, cut a strip of tape 15" long and lay it over the end of the sheet (only covering the first woven row). Cut the same notches in the tape as you did before to allow you to wrap the tape over and around the handles. Fold the tape over the sheet and onto the inside of the inner bag.

   Note: To keep it all together a little better, I rolled long strips of tape back over itself like I was making double sided tape. I lay a few across the length of the woven sheet and on the center where the bottom of the plank would sit.

2. Wrap the rest of the woven sheet down and around to the other side of the inner bag and repeat step 1.

3. To seal the four edges of the tote, you'll need four strips of tape 16" long. Trim the strip so they are only 0.75" wide. This will make it only overlap the outer strips of the woven bag and the outer strips of the side pockets, matching the rest of the project.

4. Align the edge of the strip you just made to the outer row of the woven sheet and fold it over the sidewall of the inner bag. (Make sure you cover the outer row of the pouch on the side.) Neatly tuck and fold the excess

tape hanging off the bottom edge over and under, making a nice corner.

Note: The tape you just folded over partially covers the opening to the side wall pocket. Carefully make a slit for the pocket opening and lay the rest of the tape flat.

5. Repeat steps 2–5 again for the other three remaining edges.
6. Cut two strips of tape about 0.75" × 4.5" long and repeat step 4 for the bottom edges of the pocket/woven sheet.
7. To finalize the tote, cut two strips of tape at five to 5.5" long. Align the tape to the top edge of the purse where the first strip is and fold it over to the inside of the inner bag.

Congrats! You now have a stylish, hand-woven High Quality Duct Tape Tote Bag!

100% Authentic Hoodie (110+ yd of duct tape)

By cowscankill
(http://www.instructables.com/
id/100-Authentic-Duct-Tape-
Hoodie-110-yards-of-duc/)

I was inspired to make a duct tape jacket of some kind because of hat day at my school. Why hat day, you ask? Well . . . I didn't have any awesome hats, so I made a hex hat from duct tape. It was a hit with my friends, and a lot of people gave good feedback. I was excited to do something bigger. Something with some more "wow" factor. When first worn, this jacket is kind of stiff and pretty much a plastic tube. It keeps in a *lot* of heat, and is great for wearing in the cold outside! It is also 100% waterproof, and can be

used as a rain jacket. The more you wear it, the more comfortable it gets. Unlucky for me, it is still hot here in the south, even at 5:00 a.m. when I have to go catch the bus for school.

Step 1: Materials
First, you need the right tools
- Scissors
- Razor
- Sharpie
- Yard/meter Stick

Now, gather your materials
- Duct tape. I used two 55-yard rolls, part of a 40-yard roll, and a fluorescent green tape for decorating. I probably spent around $15 for the duct tape. I didn't use professional tape—just the cheapest I could find.
- Masking tape
- A large flat surface that you can cut on. I have concrete floors, so it's no big deal. You may wish to use a large cutting board on a table if you need to (or improvise!).

Step 2: Getting Started— Duct Tape Cloth

First, we must learn how to make duct tape cloth! Making the tape can be kind of trick, but mostly just when you are covering the first layer. If two sticky parts touch in the wrong place, problems can occur. Be careful when laying down the strips! There are variations on how to make duct tape cloth, but this method works well for me and lets me get the correct size duct tape sheets I need.

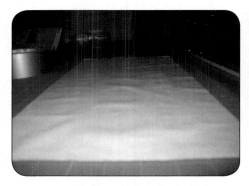

Step 3: Wait—How Big Should It Be?

On step 5, he has the measurements. Now, be careful! I used the medium measurements for the body, which is 26.75" × 24". It turns out that it is *way* too wide and the jacket will be more like a tube. It is best to make the size measurement that is closest to your size, then tailor the jacket after you finish.

Step 4: Sleeves

We need to make the sleeves. I started with the sleeves because they are the easiest. Make sure you make a plain rectangle the correct width. (Mine was 9.5"−15.35" × 21.65". 21.65" was a tad short for me. Adjust to your size.)

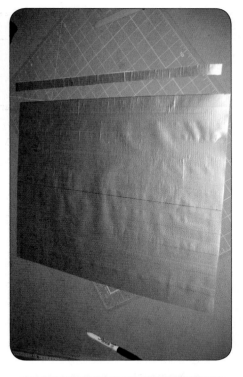

100% authentic hoodie (110+ yd of duct tape)

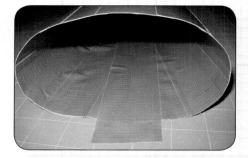

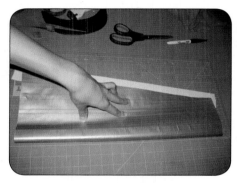

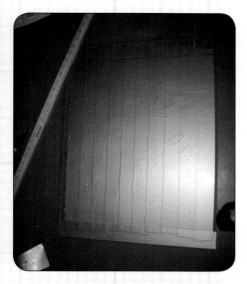

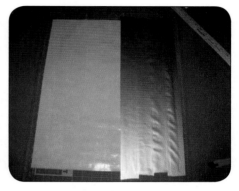

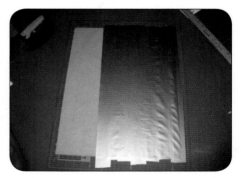

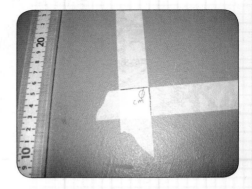

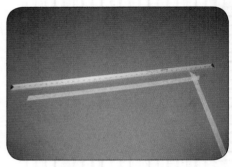

Step 5: Starting the Body

The main body is large—it did not fit on my cutting board. I used my floor to make the body, and (using masking tape, a yard stick, and a sharpie) made a large measuring angle to get the right sized duct tape cloth. If you want a zipper or a cut down the middle, make sure to measure and mark off the middle of one of the duct tape sheets.

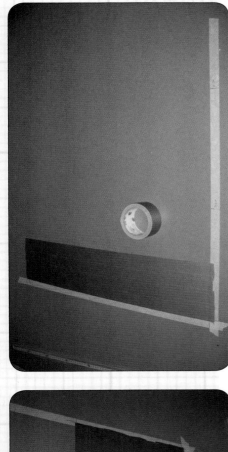

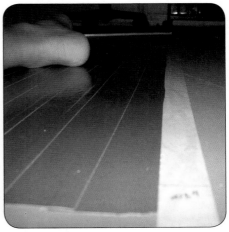

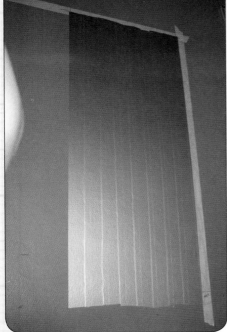

100% authentic hoodie (110+ yd of duct tape)

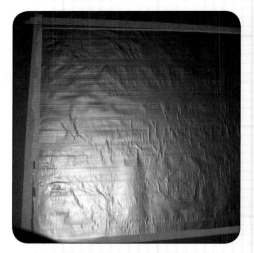

Step 6: Attaching Things

Here, we begin the end of the hoodie. The easiest way to go about attaching things is to first attach the two halves, then the sleeves, then the sides of the body. There could be another way, but I couldn't see how I was going to get duct tape strips into the enclosed area of the hoodie. The hardest part of this step is adding duct tape to the inside seem of the sleeves. It is dark inside a plastic tunnel. . . .

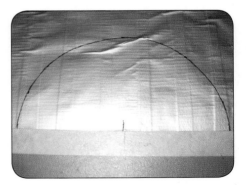

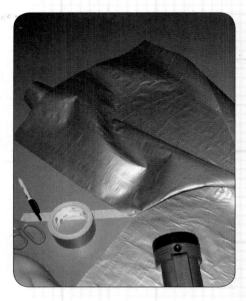

Step 7: Tailoring and Pockets!

Morning. I wake up at 5:00 a.m. to get ready for school. I decided that since I was ready early, I would tailor the jacket and make it fit better. Afternoon. Home from school, time to work on some pockets! Because they are easy! Listen to remixes of the Tetris theme.

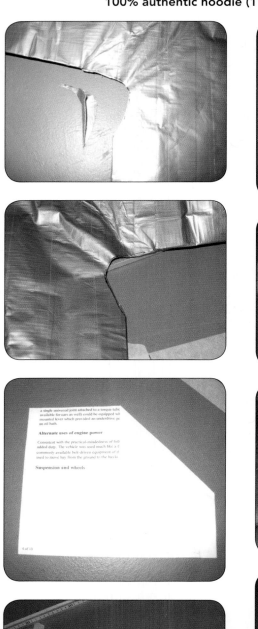

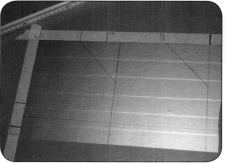

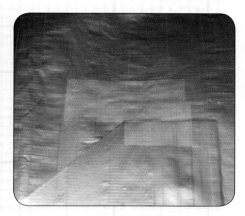

Step 8: The Long-Awaited Hood

Making the hood is pretty straightforward. All you need to do is conjoin the two rectangles and attach them to the collar of the hoodie. Trim off the top corner of the hood and round it to make it look nicer.

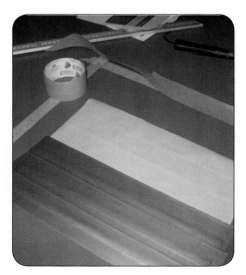

100% authentic hoodie (110+ yd of duct tape)

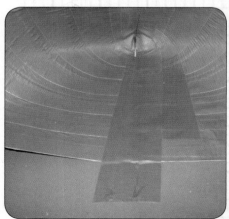

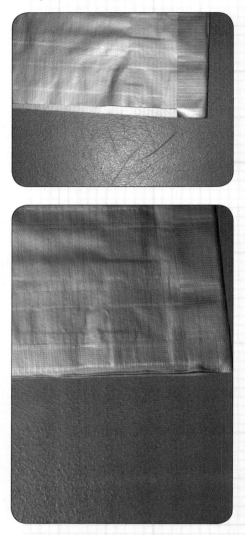

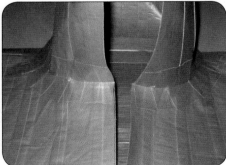

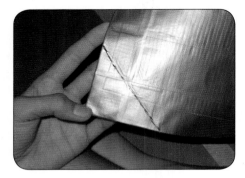

Step 9: Finishing Up!

The hoodie is technically done. But there is nothing like some colorful duct tape to make it look snazzy. You can put a bunch of stripes, checkered squares, or pictures and words with colored duct tape. I just did an easy choice and put one color of duct tape on what I consider to be borders of the jacket. After five days of work, I finished! Don't be fooled—it takes a while bit it really isn't hard. This jacket holds in a lot of heat. I mean, while taking the pictures for this in my air-conditioned room, I started sweating. It is pretty comfortable if it is cool outside with less sun. This jacket is 100% water proof also! So, if it rains while you are outside in the cold, you won't get wet! I tested this with a garden hose, and it repels very efficiently. The biggest issue is that the water drips directly onto your pants. Maybe future developments will fix this.

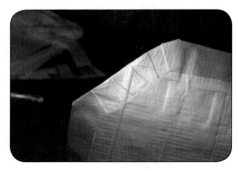

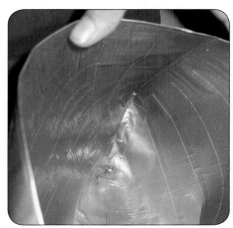

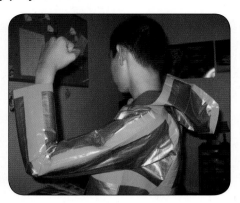

Hat

By Glenn Bukowski (oldsod)
(http://www.instructables.com/
id/Duct-Tape-Hat-3/)

Tools
- Scissors
- Stapler
- Marking pen

Supplies
- Newspaper
- Corrugated cardboard
- Two-liter soda bottle
- Rolls of duct tape (one each of silver, red, white, and blue)
- A hat to copy (I worked with a military-style cap)

The first part of the project is to develop patterns from the hat. The military-style cap I chose is simple—basically a low cylinder made from a strip of material, an oval top, and a short bill.

Start by tracing the brim onto the cardboard. If you don't have your own hat to copy, print out the pictures that I posted in this Instructable to make your own pattern (that's why I labeled them with their dimensions and photographed everything on a 1" × 1" grid).

The dimensions I used for the oval top of the hat and the two side pieces are labeled in the third picture on this page.

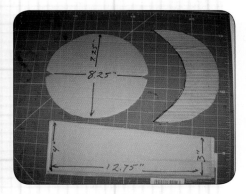

Step 1: Sheets of Silver Duct Tape

Lay strips of duct tape on the newspaper, overlapping the strips by about 0.25" to make sheets of material. One sheet will be about 9" × 10" (the top) and the other will be about 9" × 13" (the two-sided pieces). The silver duct tape will be the inside lining of your hat.

Trace the top of the hat onto the smaller piece of sheet. Notice the notches. They are there to identify the longest dimension of the oval and help you orient it when you attach it to the side of the hat. When you lay out the two side pieces, make sure that they are mirror images of each other.

Trace the bill pattern onto the side of a two-liter soda bottle with your marker and cut it out.

You'll cover the top of the plastic bill (convex side) with blue duct tape. Neatness counts!

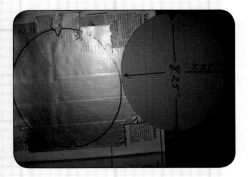

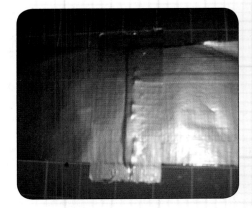

Step 2: Assemble the Sides

Now you have all the basic pieces of the hat with duct tape on one side. We'll start assembly by attaching the two side pieces together at their narrow ends. Put them together paper side (outside) to paper side then "sew" them together with a stapler.

Open them out—paper side down—and flatten the seam. Cover the stapled seam with a piece of duct tape to cover any sharp edges.

Step 3: Red, White, Blue outside

Now, the stuff that will show:

On the newspaper side of the hat, place white and red stripes of duct tape. After you've trimmed back the raw edges of the tape, place a blue strip of tape (outside hat band) at the bottom of the piece. It should overhang the sides by a little less than half its width so you can fold it over to the inside.

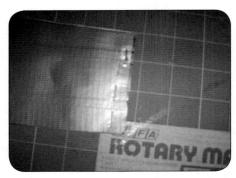

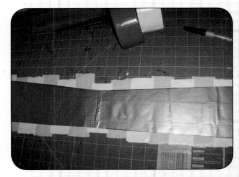

Next the top. (I covered the outside of the oval top with white tape.) Line up the notch marks of the oval with the front and back seams of the hat side and staple them in place. Then continue around the sides. (Tip: I staple halfway between the front and back staples, then halfway between the middle and the front, then halfway between that and the next, etc. Makes for neater work than trying to staple in sequence all around.)

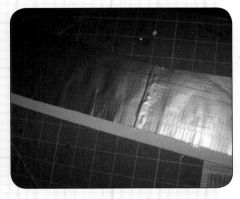

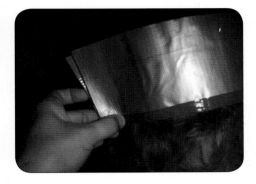

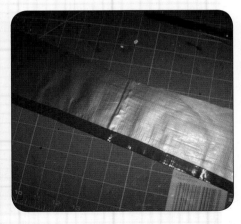

Step 4: Sizing and Assembly

Now, to the final steps:

With the side inside out, place the hat on your head and pinch the ends together to mark the seam location with your thumbnail. Staple the sides together on that pinch line. Flatten the seam out and cover it with a piece of tape.

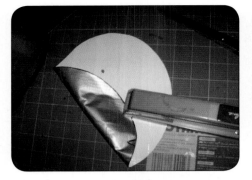

Step 6: Attach the Bill

Cover the inside of the bill (concave side) with tape. Trim the tape in front, even with the plastic form, but leave the back overhang by an inch or so. Make slits in the overhanging tape in back so it can bend up without too many wrinkles. Attach the bill to the crown of the hat, making sure the center of the bill is aligned with the front seam.

(We're almost done.)

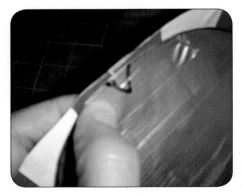

Step 5: Right-Side Out (Finally)

Now flip the hat right-side out. (So easy to say—take your time, here. This step will tell you if you have any weak points in your construction.) You start with the silver side out, end up with the red, white, and blue side out.

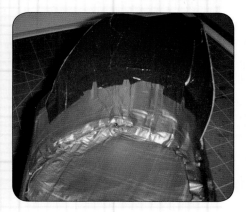

Step 7: Final Assembly

Cut a 24" strip of tape and fold it a half-inch or so over, this will be the inner hat band. Middle the tape and start attaching it to the hat from the center front to the back on one side, then the other. You should have some overlap at the back of the hat.

Try it on. If your hat feels too loose, you can add another layer of tape to the inside hat band.

OPTIONAL STEPS

You can put a decoration on the top. (I made a star from blue tape—too much white showing otherwise.)

You might want to take a leather punch and cut some vent holes around the side. Remember that duct tape is waterproof and a little air-flow is a good thing.

Step 8: FINISHED!

The tie-dye hat is the one I made for my wife. Try one and use your imagination for color combos!

I just bought four rolls of duct tape, and needed something to do with it. My little brother was bugging my dad for a new 3DS case, so a little light bulb went off in my head, and I got right to work! Average time: 45 min–1 hr.

Step 1: Materials
You will need

- A primary duct tape color (referred to here on in as Tape A)
- A secondary duct tape color (referred to here on in as Tape B)
- Console, games, and, in this case, a stylus
- Pen and paper
- Velcro dots (two is enough)
- OPTIONAL: something to cut the tape with. I used my hands and found it to be easier.

Step 2: Take Some Measurements

Make some measurements of whatever you need to hold. Try to keep it wider rather than thinner, so there's a little wiggle room. The stylus is not as important, as we will only make a small holster/slot for it.

Step 3:

Use enough of Tape A to cover about 2.5 times the length (top to bottom) of the console, and make a sort of "cloth." Five pieces were enough for me. Don't worry about the ends not being perfect, we'll cover those up later. Place more tape on the cloth, sticky side to sticky side, to make a duct tape cloth, so to speak. Then, fold lengths of Tape B over the sides to A) cover up the ragged edges and B) make it look cool. It should loosely hold the console folded over, with plenty of overhang.

Step 4: Make Game Slots

Make a small piece of duct tape loosely the dimensions of the game, with about the width of two pennies on any side. Then, use a larger piece to cover it. There should be a U-shape of stickiness around a cloth portion. Stick that on the case, with the open end at the top. Continue until you reach the desired number of slots. My brother wanted six, so I made six slots in a 3" × 2" rectangle.

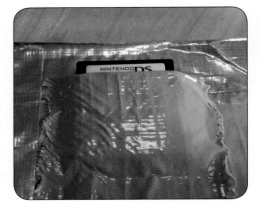

Step 6: Add Tape and Attach

Put some of Tape B on all but one long side of the newly made cloth, as depicted. Fold the tape over on the body to attach the pocket to the body. This is where the console goes.

Step 5: Make Another Cloth Section

This one took me about two pieces lengthwise. Make it about 0.5" longer than the body on each side.

Step 7: OPTIONAL: Stylus Holder

Make a thin strip of tape (use the width of the roll as a length guide. 0.5" should be enough. Then, make another about 0.75" in length. Stick the small one sticky side to sticky side on the other. Stick it to the main pocket. I made two.

Step 8: Add a Little Flair

Down the middle, over Tape A, put a length of Tape B. Don't cover the edges (already covered with Tape B). Over those edges, cover with Tape A. Use the picture as a guide.

Step 9: Add Velcro Dots/ Strips

This is to ensure that nothing falls out. Note: Put the first dot on the top so you don't accidentally cover up the game pocket like I did.

Step 10: Final Product!

Fill the case with your swag and it's done! Also available in PSP flavor.

Stars and Stripes Lawn Chair

By Kapaow
(http://www.instructables.com/
id/Stars-and-Stripes-Duct-Tape-
Lawn-Chair/)

We decided to fix up my grandmother's old lawn chair for the 3M Duct Tape Contest.

Step 1: Clean Up the Chair

Cut off all the old straps and wipe off the aluminum with a damp rag.

Step 2: Preparation

We used a rust-proof, hammered-bronze spray paint finish. We applied several thin coats, making sure it did not run.

Step 3: Making the Straps

Measure the width of the chair and add about 3", which will allow 1.5" on each side for the tape to wrap around the post. Stick it, sticky side up to two secure places (not on the chair). This step is to layer the tape to make it strong enough to sit on and to cover the sticky side. Make sure it's tight. Then place another layer of tape (sticky side to sticky side, leaving 1.5" on each end uncovered) on top of the strips. Make sure it is aligned correctly. Once centered, slowly run your finger along the tape to stick them together. Be sure to remove as many air bubbles as possible. Repeat this step on the top and bottom to attain the desired strength. (More layers equal more strength and less stretch.) We did three layers.

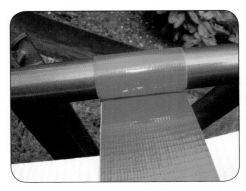

Step 4: Putting It Together

We did all the red, horizontal strips first, and then we wove the white and one blue strip through them. Make sure your straps are tight and evenly spaced. All vertical straps go under the metal bar in the back.

Step 5: FINISHED

We can't wait to present our grandmother with her "new" duct tape chair on the Fourth of July so she can sit and enjoy the fireworks in stars and stripes style!

Duct Duck (Duck Tub Stopper)

By Kate Jackson
(shesparticular)
(http://www.instructables.com/
id/Duct-Duck-Duct-Tape-Duck-
Tub-Stopper/)

Duct tape is truly magical. It can be used for nearly everything, including creating an awesome little ducky which can then be attached to a tub stopper to make taking a bath super fun!

Step 1: You'll Need
- Duct tape (I'm using yellow, but you can use whatever color you like)
- Scissors
- Grommet tool and grommet
- Hole punch or leather punch
- Tub stopper
- Thin chain (approximately 10")
- Two coins or other small weights (I used pennies)
- Pliers (optional but suggested)

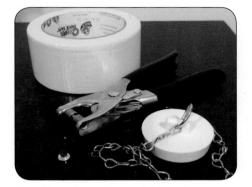

Step 2: Making Duct Tape Sheets

Before we can get to the folding process to create a duck, we'll need to make some duct tape sheets.

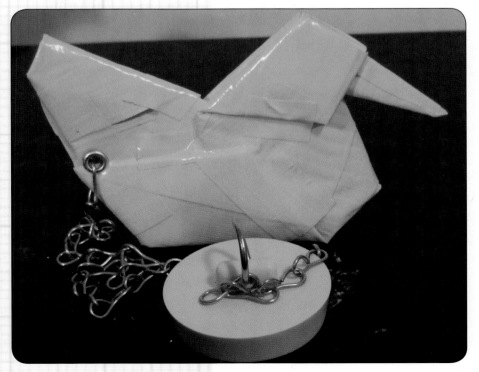

duct duck (duck tub stopper)

Cut a piece of duct tape approximately 9" long and place it sticky side up on your work surface. Cut two more pieces the same length and place them over the first so that they meet at its center. Flip the whole thing over and apply pieces to cover the outside edges. Repeat until you have roughly a square of duct tape sheet. Trim the sheet down to form an 8.5" × 8.5" square

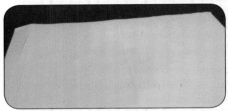

Step 3: Get Ready to Spread Your Wings

Fold in two sides of the sheet to the center to form a kite shape. Then, fold the long point back to meet the shorter point. After that, fold the long point back again so that the fold is even with the layers underneath. Fold in the shorter point so that the tip meets the layers underneath. Then, fold the long point under itself to form a beak. When that's finished, lift the entire thing up and fold it in half to form two halves of a duck. Pull the neck and head portions out slightly and crease them into place. Fold the bottom portion on each side up to form the base of the body. Fold the flaps at the back of the body inside to form the tail portion. Position the coins under the body portion of the duck (on the inside) and cover each with a piece of tape. These will help ensure your ducky doesn't take a header when placed in water. Cut small pieces of tape and apply it to any areas that may need some help staying held together.

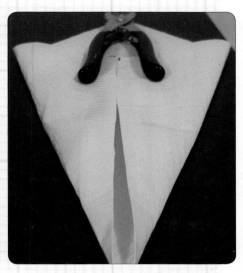

Step 4: Duct Duck . . . Goose?

You can skip this step if you just want to make a duct tape ducky, but making it into a bath stopper is even more fun!

Punch a hole in the back portion of the duck using a leather punch or hole punch. Using a grommet tool, add a grommet to the hole. Connect the duck to the tub stopper using the chain. Fill your tub, add bubbles, and hop in!

Tear-Away Scratch Pad

By wonderfulone
(http://www.instructables.com/
id/Duct-Tape-Tear-Away-Scratch-
Pad/)

Convert scrap paper into a handy notepad with tear-away sheets using duct tape instead of specialty binding glue.

What you'll need

- Scrap paper
- Cereal box or other cardboard for backing
- Duct tape
- Binder clips or rubber bands
- Glue stick
- Paper cutter
- Scissors

Step 1: Cut Your Paper and Backing

Using a paper cutter of your choice (swing arm, rotary, etc.), cut your scrap paper and backing to desired size. When you are stacking the paper after it is cut, be sure to stack so that the side to be bound consists of uncut edges. This step isn't absolutely necessary, but I have found that uncut edges are easier to align and adhere better. I chose to make mostly 5.5" × 8.5" and 5.5" × 4.25" notepads. I also made one 4" by 2.5" mini notepad. You can also leave the paper uncut if you prefer a full size scratch pad.

wrinkles and seep between the pages, causing them to stick together.

Step 3: Bind your Pages

Cut a length of tape slightly longer than the width of the edge to be bound. If you are making a notepad that is thicker than the width of your tape, use several strips positioned side by side. With the back of your notebook facing up, position the tape so there is enough overhang to cover the thickness of the pad. It is better to have too much overhang than too little, the excess can always be cut away. Press down on the backing to secure the tape, then flip the pad over. Starting from the middle, pull the tape upwards, while putting downward pressure on the pages, before smoothing the tape along the edge. Continue this motion outwards toward the edges until the width of the notebook has been secured with tape. Smooth down the taped edge, ensuring even adhesion. Cut way any excess tape.

Step 2: Prep your Pages

Once all your pages and backings are cut, align the edge to be bound until it is as smooth as possible. Any pages that are not aligned correctly will not adhere to the tape. Use binder clips or rubber bands to keep the pages and backing in place. Apply a thin layer of glue using a glue stick to help keep pages together while you apply the duct tape and to add a little extra stickiness. Do not use liquid glue; it will create

at least one straight side is possible (triangles, hearts). If you're particularly ambitious, you could try circles, stars, anything really

Before binding your pages, use a hole punch or a decorative punch to create an easy way to hang a scratch pad on a nail or thumb tack.

Print lines or a decorative header on pages before cutting and binding them, making your own custom stationary.

Apply a magnetic strip to the back of the scratch pad and hang it on the fridge for grocery lists.

Step 4: Other Ideas...

Rectangular or square notepads are easiest to make, but any shape with

Homemade Rockets

Not just a rocket in your pocket, but an entire rocket factory and launch system!

Step 1: Materials

The materials are easy to find in most modern homes:

- A pocket-sized box
- A box of matches
- A small scrap of wood
- Some pieces of kitchen foil
- Optional extra: a pocket lighter.

Step 2: Making the Launch Pad

Take the scrap of wood and trim it to fit inside the box. Halfway along it, drill a small hole at an angle of 45°—the hole needs to be just large enough to fit a matchstick into.

Step 3: Outfitting the Kit

Er, well, you just put it all in the box. . . . If you put the pieces of foil at the bottom, they'll stay flatter.

Step 4: Making and Launching a Rocket

Take one piece of foil and lay two matches head-to-head at one end. Roll the matches up in the foil. Make sure that one match can slide out of the foil tube you've made, though not too easily. Twist the foil tightly around the other match. Slot the rocket into the launcher and apply heat to the middle of the foil, either with another match or with the lighter. After a few moments, the heat conducted by the foil will light the match-heads, and . . . *woosh!* . . . off it will go.

I could make a lot of fuss about health and safety, but if you're old enough to be allowed to play with matches, you're old enough to know where and when you should launch rockets like this. If you set fire to the cat and burn down the garden, it's your own fault.

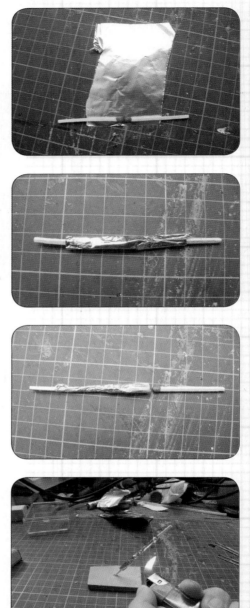

Ten-Minute Rocket

By: (zack)
(http://www.instructables.com/
id/10-Minute-Rocket/)

This Instructable will teach you how to build a simple, ultra-light rocket from household items (and of course a rocket engine). Here's the supply list:

- 1 tube of superglue
- 1 roll of tinfoil
- 1 straw big enough to fit around your launch rod
- 1 deck of playing cards that you don't mind parting with
- 1 C rocket engine
- Several rocket engine detonators and plugs
- 1 electronic detonator (and necessary cables)

WARNING: This is totally dangerous. I didn't die, but you might. It is *not my fault* if you hurt yourself following these instructions.

Step 1: Building Yourself Some Fins

The fins themselves are pretty simple: the difficult part is positioning them evenly around the rocket. To make a fin, first you'll need to fold a playing card in half hamburger style. Take your superglue

and seal the folded halves together, like a sandwich. Glue is going to ooze out the sides and get all over your fingers Suck it up and take it like a man. Make two of these sandwiches and let the glue completely dry. Now you need to do a little bit of measuring, but nothing too complicated. Take one of the folded cards and put it perpendicular to the other, forming an L. Mark off the edge and cut it away so you're left with one square-ish shape. Repeat with the other folded card and, if you've done everything correctly thus far, you should be left with two pseudo-squares. Take these faux-squares and cut diagonally across from the curved corner to the corner directly opposite. You should now have four fin shapes, congratulations. Now onto the difficult part: attaching them.

Step 2: Attaching the Fins

Basically, you want the fins to be completely perpendicular to each other. I realize that this is darn near impossible; but if you somehow screw up the positioning horribly, the rocket could possibly come back and hit you in the face. Take your time. I've attached a template PDF to the end of this Instructable; I would recommend printing it out and using it as a guide when you're gluing. Superglue is really *really* good at bonding cardboard, so you're only going to get one shot at this. Line up your engine, apply a small amount of glue to the edge of the fin, and take the dive. The first fin is the easiest, but every other fin has to be positioned as accurately as possible to prevent the rocket from spinning out. Again, just take your time and it should be fine. Once you have all the fins loosely attached, apply a liberal amount of glue to the seams. You do not want one of these falling off mid flight. Put the rocket in the sun to dry; the next step is going to take a while.

Step 3: Sculpting a Nose Cone

Take a large piece of aluminum foil, about 5" by 5", and begin to shape it into a cone. This step is a little tricky and takes a bit of practice, but you'll probably get it after your third or fourth failed cone. You'll want to rub it on a smooth surface to work out all the kinks, and over time (with liberal amounts of elbow grease) the cone should begin to take shape. Be sure to check that the tip is centered after every few minutes of honing; if it is skewed it could also affect the trajectory of your rocket. Once you're satisfied with your cone, just glue it onto the end of your rocket. Mine happened to fit perfectly within the cardboard tube, but it's fine if yours is a bit larger. I applied a good puddle of glue around the cone and waited for it to harden, just to ensure the cone was attached snugly.

Step 4: Attaching the Launch Lug

Cut a piece of straw about the length of your rocket's body. Carefully glue it between two of your fins, and position it parallel to the body. Wait for it to dry, and then again apply more glue. You don't want this one to fall off either: it's a pretty crucial part of the rocket. Once your launch lug is dried on, you're all done. Find a good open area to launch it and prepare the detonator.

Step 5: LAUNCH

Carefully insert the detonator and seal the hole with a plug. Clip the leads onto the ends of the detonator and tilt the launch pad away from you at about a 45° angle. Step back, and press the button. If all goes according to plan, the rocket should shoot off the launch pad and fly pretty darn far.

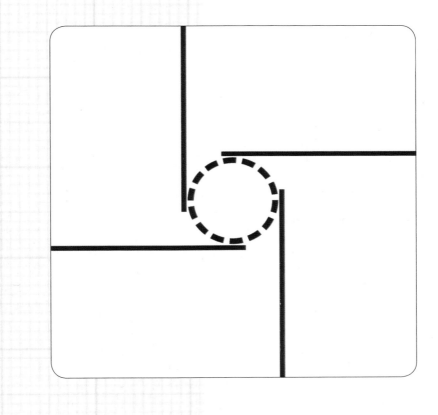

Compressed Air Rockets

By: Mike Warren
(mikeasaurus)
(http://www.instructables.com/
id/compressed-air-rockets/)

When I was at the Bay Area Maker Faire earlier this year, I saw a display that had a compressed air paper rocket launcher. Kids would make their own paper rockets, load them onto a launching tube, and fire them into the sky. I thought it was pretty cool, but I wanted something more dangerous different.

So, how do you make compressed air rockets better? By making exploding compressed air paper rockets!

Using simple Chinatown fireworks, combined with an elastic deployment system to eject a small toy parachute action figure, I designed a rocket that jettisons the parachute man from altitude. I made three test rockets, which were designed to test and calibrate the compressed air launcher and six live rockets, which were intended to test the theory and intent of my design. Unfortunately, it didn't quite turn out the way it was supposed to. All six live rockets exploded, melted, or malfunctioned and no parachute men were successfully deployed.

So, instead of this being a how-to, it's more of a how-not-to.

Obviously working with fireworks, compressed air, power tools, and rockets is dangerous business. Use common sense and work within your ability.

Enough talk: let's explode some rockets!

Step 1: Tools and Materials

Tools
- Hacksaw
- Wood saw
- Drill and bits (various sizes, wood bits)
- Scissors
- Hobby knife
- PVC glue
- Lighter
- Masking tape
- Bicycle pump

Materials
- PVC pipe
- 1 × 2" diameter pipe (roughly 24" long)
- 1 × 2" cap
- 1 × 2" diameter to 1.5" diameter bushing
- 2 × 1" threaded coupler
- 1 × 1" diameter pipe (roughly 24" long)
- Launch platform
- Scrap wood uprights
- Scrap ¼" plywood base
- Scrap 2"×4" for blocking
- Scrap 2"×4" for launcher stabilizer
- Sprinkler valve (1" ingress/egress)
- Compressed air-gun trigger
- Schrader valve (inner tube valve)
- Paper

- Cardboard/card stock
- Elastic bands
- Threaded rod and wingnut
- Cable ties

Step 2: Launcher—Overview

All compressed air rocket launchers work under the principle of rapidly displacing air to launch a projectile. Air can be pressurized in a chamber and then deployed by means of a trigger or stored in a bladder and squeezed to be released. These are active and passive systems.

Active or pressurized assemblies are capable of producing some spectacular results due to the high pressure able to be stored in the chamber. Passive systems like stomp rockets reply on the pressure created when the air bladder is squeezed. This project focuses on the former.

The setup of this pressurized air launcher is simple:

- Air is supplied through a bicycle pump attached to the intake nipple.
- Air is held in the pressure chamber until it is released by the trigger.
- The trigger is attached to a modified sprinkler valve (pilot valve).
- When the trigger is activated, air is released through the exhaust.

Keen observers of Instructables. com may recognize this canon as Fungus Amungus' Christmas canon. This is the same canon but adapted to fit on a launching pad. And this version shoots exploding rockets—not confetti.

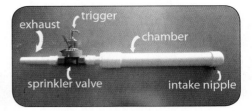

Step 3: Launcher—Detail
Chamber

This canon was made with about 28" of 2" PVC pipe as the chamber. Cut your 2" pipe to length and glue on the 2" cap to one of the ends. On the other end, glue on the 2" to 1" bushing. Then, cut a 4–6" length of 1" PVC and glue that into the bushing. Finally, glue the 1" threaded coupler onto the 1" pipe attached to the bushing. Set chamber assembly aside for 24 hours until glue has cured. Once set, drill an opening in the cap for the Schrader valve. Tap the opening and wrap the valve in Teflon tape and screw it into the opening.

Sprinkler Valve

I did not perform the modifications to this valve. It appears that the valve has had the electronic solenoid removed and replaced with the handle and trigger for a compressed air nozzle. The trigger is threaded and fits directly into the place where the solenoid trigger was. Replacing the electronic portion was a simple mechanical action. The valve is 1" female threaded on both ends.

Exhaust

Cut a length of 12" to 14" of 1" PVC pipe, then glue the threaded couple to one end. Set aside to dry.

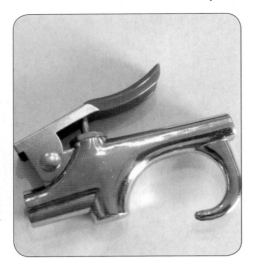

layers of masking tape. The masking tape allows the rocket to withstand the pressure when the PVC pipe is filled with air, and the card stock provides a rigid flat base for the rest of the payload to be built upon.

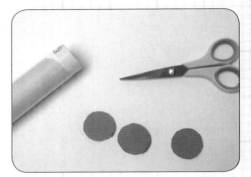

Step 5: Rocket Assembly— Payload

The payload is the trickiest part of the assembly, and errors here are probably what brought my project to failure.

Lower Assembly (Charge)

After the fuselage was completed, a short cylinder of card stock was installed on top of the bottom deck previously installed. The cylinder was secured with plenty of masking tape, and a firework was installed inside. Notches were made in two places on the top portion of the cylinder after its installation: one at the location where the firework will explode/emit flame and another off to the side, which will allow the fuse to pass through and be lit once the assembly is closed.

With the firework installed, another circle of card stock was covered in

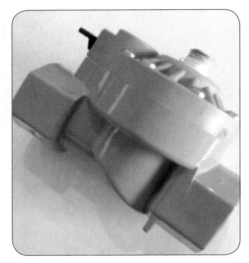

Step 4: Rocket Assembly— Fuselage

Time to make our rockets! Take an A4 (8.5" × 11") sheet of paper and roll it lengthwise, using a 1" PVC pipe as our frame. When the paper has been completely rolled tape the length with masking tape.

Next, cover the top of the paper with a cardboard or card stock circle roughly the same size as the pipe (1" diameter). Then secure it in place using several

aluminum foil and installed over the cylinder opening. More masking tape was used to secure the charge in place, ensuring that the notched openings created earlier weren't covered.

Upper Assembly (Parachute Man)

Another longer card stock cylinder was made and attached to the lower assembly in just one small area using masking tape, making the top cylinder hinged. This hinge will allow the payload to open when ignited and the brave parachute soldier will be deployed. Well, that was the idea. The top of the upper assembly was capped with another circle of card stock, then a parachute soldier was inserted into the assembly. Close the upper assembly and use a single strip of masking tape over the notch made earlier for the firework explosion point. A cone of paper was added to the top after the payload was finished.

Elastic Mechanism

To allow the upper assembly to flap open when the masking tape strap was severed, an elastic was used. Cut a rubber band and fix one end to the upper assembly, pull taught, and fix the other end to the base of the fuselage. I used masking tape to secure the elastic in place.

Step 6: Launch Platform

Since I was going to be filming, lighting fireworks, and pulling the compressed air trigger, I needed a platform to hold the launcher. I made this launch platform in less than an hour with scrap wood hanging around the shop. This platform is made from a 12" × 12" × ½" sheet of plywood, a drawer face that measured 6" × 48" × ½", and some 2" × 4" off-cuts of various lengths.

A threaded rod was installed near the top and through a 2" × 4", which allows the launcher to be directed at an angle. You know, in case I wanted to launch exploding rockets at the neighbors and not just straight up. Holes were drilled into the top movable

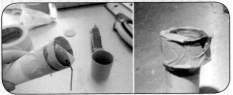

platform, which the launcher will be strapped to with cable ties.

could be damaged, and this should be definitely be undertaken by someone who knows what they are doing. Not heeding my own advice, I launched from the roof of the Instructables.com lab in downtown San Francisco.

Here's a few images from rockets 1–3 shown from different angles.

Step 7: Launch!

With the assembly done, it's time to test the rockets out. You should probably launch someplace that is wide-open and has no people or buildings nearby that

Step 8: Results

My measure of success for this project was successful deployment of the parachute soldier at altitude. To that end, this project did not work as intended. However, it was loads of fun to make, and any project I can walk away from with all my fingers should be seen as a positive learning experience.

That's it, get outside and fire off some rockets. Be safe and have fun!

Paper Stomp Rockets

By: seamster
(http://www.instructables.com/
id/Paper-Stomp-Rockets-Easy-
and-Fun/)

I run a free summertime activity program for kids as part of my job in the city where I live. So I've got a lot of fun little projects up my sleeves, and I'm always on the lookout for more. One of the more popular summertime activities in my repertoire is homemade stomp rockets. Stomp rockets are great because they are both creative and physical.

There are many versions of paper stomp rockets and launchers out there. They all work essentially the same way: Air is forced through a PVC contraption, which launches a lightweight paper rocket up into the air. This particular launcher design is a combination of a handful of ideas I've seen, along with a few of my own additions.

I have a basic rocket design that I drew up that uses a single sheet of paper, which I've included as a PDF at the end of this Instructable.

Read on, and then go have some fun.

Step 1: Materials

This launcher design produces no waste, and should cost around $10.

For One Launcher
- One 10' length of ½" PVC
- One ½" 90° elbow (all fittings are of the slip variety)
- One ½" four-way fitting
- Two ½" end caps
- One 1" coupling
- One 1" × ½" bushing
- One 2-liter soda bottle cap
- Lots of 2-liter soda bottles

Other Necessary Supplies
- PVC cement
- Hot glue
- White glue
- Cotton balls
- Tape
- Sheets of 8.5" × 11" paper
- Lots of copies of the attached PDF rocket template

Step 2: Cut the PVC

From your 10' length of PVC, cut the following pieces:

- One 40" piece
- One 18" piece
- One 5" piece
- Two 12" pieces
- Three 11" pieces

Of all the pieces to be cut, accuracy is the most crucial on the three 11" pieces. These will be made into forming tubes, which will be used to help make the actual rockets. Construction of the forming tubes is covered in Step 5.

Step 3: Build Basic Launcher Assembly

The photos should provide enough detail on how to construct the basic launcher assembly. Use PVC cement to put it all together.

The 12" pieces are the side supports that make the base. The 18" piece is the riser from which the rockets will launch. I used my palm sander to quickly knock off the sharp edge of the launch-end of the 18" piece of PVC.

The 1" coupling and the 1" × ½" bushing go together to make the bottle end of the launcher.

Step 4: Make the Bottle End of the Launcher

Two-liter bottles make great bladders for stomp rocket launchers because they're readily available and they're pretty durable. This set-up is especially nice because it allows you to quickly replace bottles when they've been completely worn out or cracked.

Begin by drilling a hole through a 2-liter bottle cap. This is easiest to do while the cap is screwed onto an old bottle.

I prefer to use hot glue to glue the bottle cap into the opening of the 1" coupling. Hot glue is quick, fills the gap between the bottle cap and coupling nicely, and is only semi-permanent.

When the bottle cap itself begins to wear out and the threads are stripped, you can just grab it with a pair of pliers and yank it out to replace it with a new one.

Step 5: Make Rocket Forming Tubes

The three 11" pieces of PVC will be used to make three separate rocket forming tubes. These will help you make perfect rockets every time. It's nice to have a few on hand so more than one person can be working on a rocket at the same time.

You want the forming tubes to be slightly bigger than the tube that the rockets get launched from. This is accomplished by gluing a sheet of 8.5" × 11" paper around each forming tube. I used white glue and glued each sheet directly to the tube, and then to itself after rolling it on tightly.

A piece of tape (I used electrical tape) was wrapped around one end of each paper-covered tube. This is to aid in the construction of the rocket, as detailed in the next step.

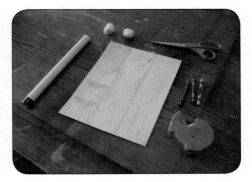

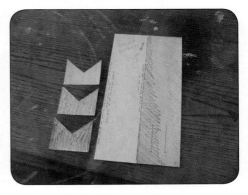

Step 6: Make Some Rockets

Print out and make plenty of copies of the attached PDF rocket template. There are basic building instructions on the rocket template. Decorate and cut out areas as directed.

Roll the rocket body section onto a forming tube, with the bottom of rocket (where the fin placement lines are located) just above the tape at the end of the forming tube. This creates an open space at the top of the tube where the cotton balls will go.

Tape the body tube together, but *not* to the forming tube. Fold the fins and tape them in place on the fin placement lines. Place two cotton balls into the open area at the top of the paper tube, and cover with a couple of pieces of tape. Remove the rocket from forming tube.

I have made a total of six launchers, a couple of which were made with 45° angled risers. These have been especially fun.

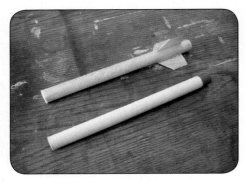

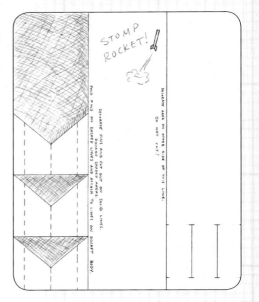

Step 7: Launch!

Before you launch your rockets, be sure to explain some safety rules to everyone involved so nobody gets shot in the eye.

After each launch, you will have to refill the bottle with air. I tell the kids to hold the top of the launch tube with their hand and blow through their hand to fill up the bottle. This way, germ-passing is somewhat minimized.

Vacuum-Cleaner Bazooka

By: ynze
(http://www.instructables.com/
id/Make-a-Vacuum-cleaner-
Bazooka/)

In five minutes, you can build an air-powered bazooka. The bazooka launches plastic capsules about 100 feet. And with some tweaking, you might stretch that distance quite a bit.

Step 1: Stuff You Need

- A vacuum cleaner (any model will do)
- Straight piece of PVC tube, at least 1 meter long with a 35 mm inner diameter. Longer is better (see the text on tweaking)!
- A PVC three-way junction with an angle of 45° that fits the straight PVC tube.
- Duct tape
- A projectile: I used the plastic capsule that is inside "surprise-eggs" (see picture). Old school film containers work as well. Whatever you use, make sure that the projectile's diameter is just a little smaller than the PVC tubes'.
- A small piece of cardboard (business cards are perfect).

Step 2: Make It

Attach the three-way junction to the straight tube using duct tape (you can glue the parts with PVC glue, of course, but there's no good reason to do so). Wrap duct tape around the tip of the vacuum cleaners' hose, so that it fits snugly into the slanting tube. This fit should be as air-tight as possible. Push the vacuum-cleaners' hose into the slanting tube of the PVC junction

177

part. Test whether the projectile can run smoothly through the assembled PVC tubes when the vacuum-cleaner is attached.

Step 3: Launch It and Tweak It
Launch It

Power up the vacuum cleaner. Cover the tubes' ending with the PVC-junction with the business card. The vacuum cleaner will now suck air from the other end of the PVC tube. Hold the projectile firmly, and insert it in the air-sucking tip of the PVC tube. Let go and enjoy!

Tweak It

If you extend the straight PVC tube, the projectile will be accelerated over a longer period. And so the projectile's velocity will increase. So extend that piece of tube! Add some weight to the projectile. We filled the capsule with rice, but sand might work better. Experiment to find the right weight for the projectile. Again: Have fun! Also, be careful and don't shoot in the direction of living creatures.

I've seen all sorts of water bottle rockets on Instructables and while surfing the web, but I thought an Instructable with the step-by-step process of building a whole bunch of them with a class of grade six kids would be good. Each step in the Instructable will be a day in the class. At the top of each day, you'll find a list of tools and materials. Just follow through a day in advance and you'll have kids learning so much more than anyone bargained for.

This rocket is based on the usual 2-liter pop bottle you find at grocery stores. You add water and pressurized air and, using these instructions, you'll get height that you and your students will not believe. To make it interesting, we have a passenger . . . the Eggstronaut. This is an egg that, if it survives, will award extra marks to the team.

You'll need the basic materials listed below as well as a launcher. A good hand pump works, well but a compressor *really* makes life easy. You can maximize the pressure like crazy, too.

Learning Objectives:

- The students will learn and apply Newton's Second Law of Motion in a way that makes sense to them.
- "The more massive an object is . . . the more force it takes to accelerate it." Or you could say, "Heavy stuff takes more force to move."

- The students will learn and apply the basic principles of Newton's Third Law of Motion. "To every action there is an equal and opposite reaction." Or you could say, "If you push something, it will push back."
- The students will understand Newton's First Law of Motion: "F=MA." Or, to make it so I can understand, "Stuff that is sitting there will stay that way unless something happens to it. Once things start moving, they tend to keep moving until something happens to change how it is moving."
- Students will learn to tell the difference between *mass* and *size*.
- By building a simple rocket, the students will understand these laws in a way that makes sense to them. They will also learn to think creatively, design, and

problem solve while building a basic design.

- The students will learn to use basic tools to construct a working project.

Tools and Materials:

- Scissors
- Hot glue gun
- Duct tape
- X-acto or Olfa mat knife
- 2-liter pop bottles (*not* water bottles!). Get at least two of them.
- Cardboard or coroplast (the stuff cheap signs are made of)
- Batting, foam, paper strips (whatever you find for the Eggstronaut)
- egg

Vocabulary:

- **Pressurizing**
- **Ratio**
- **Symmetrical**
- **Hypotenuse**
- **Scale** (as in drawing to scale)

I'll also provide a marking sheet at the end so you can use it in your class.

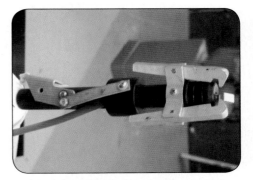

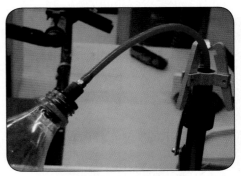

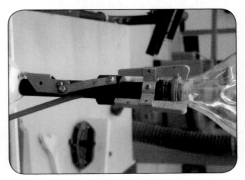

Step 1: Day 1—The Introduction

Tools and Materials:

- A couple of 2-liter bottles
- Big sheets of paper (I cut stuff off a roll from the art guys.)
- Metersticks or yardsticks
- Lots of pencils
- An egg
- A computer with examples of water-bottle rockets from the web (check out YouTube)

After you show the kids examples from the web they will be hard to hold back. It's pretty cool. I start asking questions like these:

- How does it fly?
- Why are some short and some long?
- Some rockets have two fins, some have six. Why?
- What about the fin size?

I cover each of these points on the board. What you want to coax out of them is: The rockets fly by pressurizing air with water. This is important because the "booster bottle," which is pressurized, *must* be a bottle for carbonated drinks and *must not* be punctured or cut *at all*. It will explode if otherwise. I've done it and it is really scary. Funny, but scary.

Long rockets (double length) work best. You can chat about what **ratio** is now. Suggest methods of lengthening the rocket (tubes, extra bottles, etc.).

Two to four fins that are **symmetrical** work best. Keep them small and explain that, because the rockets explode off at more than 100kph, large fins will rip off. A good size is a triangle with **hypotenuse** of 3–7" and bottom edge of 1–3".

Now introduce the Eggstronaut. Explain that, if the passenger survives, they will get extra marks. They love this. Go over padding and protection if you want, but I find the kids come up with the most amazing ideas . . . better than mine! My only stipulation is that they have to make an escape hatch that can be used to insert and remove the Eggstronaut on the field.

Once the kids are ready, I break them into groups of two or three. Don't do four . . . you always get at least one kid who is left in the cold. I pull out the paper and teach them about drawing objects to scale on the paper. You can trace out a bottle or two to help them visualize it.

Spend the remaining time working on design. You'll get a couple groups that finish the drawing in minutes. Just send them back with revisions, measurements, notes, or whatever you can make up. Make sure they draw the fins to size and that they are being realistic about the egg and how it will get into the hatch.

Spend some time discussing materials. I ask the kids to bring bottles, long cardboard tubes, cardboard, coroplast, and any packing material they will need. It's up to you. I supply basic tools and tape to build the rocket with.

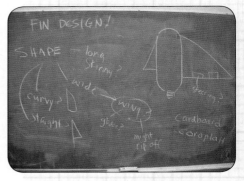

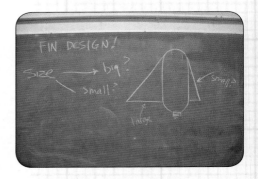

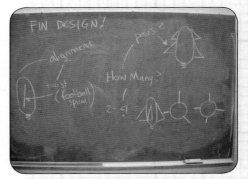

Step 2: Day 2—Building and Newton's Second and Third Laws

Tools and Materials:

- Duct tape
- Hot glue and hot gue guns (optional)
- 2-liter bottles
- Cardboard and coroplast
- Scissors, X-acto knife, mat knifes, etc.
- Material for batting
- 2 skateboards (if you can find them)

The kids are ready to build, but first you can do a fun demo. The first law I teach about is Newton's 2nd Law: "The more massive an object is . . . the more force it takes to accelerate it." In other words, "Heavy stuff takes more force to move."

I like to demonstrate this by pulling up the smallest kid in the class. I pull out two skateboards, facing each other and about 2' apart. I put the student on one skateboard and I stand on the other. I'm not a big guy, but usually the size discrepancy is pretty obvious. I longboard as a hobby, but I act like I've never stood on one. I ask the student to hold out both hands in front, and I do the same. I ask the class what would happen if we pushed our hands together really hard. Of course, the kids know what happens, so I gently push on the hands of the student. It's amazing how far a kid will roll. I won't move more than a couple of inches.

I get the kids to notice two things.

- The person with less mass moved further
- The person with more mass still moved a little bit.

Newton's 2nd law relates to the idea that objects with more mass will take more energy to accelerate or move. The person with less mass moved more because it takes less energy to move them. The other part of the demo is that the person with more mas still moved.

This is explained by Newtons 3rd law which says: "To every action, there is an equal and opposite reaction." In other words, "if you push something, it will push back."

The kids notice that I move as well. You could explain the idea that, every time objects move each other, *both* have the same force being pushed on them. Objects with more mass don't *move* as much, but they still have the same energy exerted on them. This is also a good explanation for why we add water to the bottle. The water being pushed out from the bottle has more mass than air, so it pushes against the bottle harder, which forces the bottle up with more force. You can tie this into Newton's 2nd law as well if the kids are still engaged at this point.

Now you can start building stuff! Pull out the drawings, gather the materials, and demonstrate a couple of skills.

Stacking Bottles for Height

Show how to cut a bottle safely with a blade. Keep the cap on when starting (makes it easier). I cut a bottle open about 4" up from the bottom and then show how they can stack. It's up to you if you want the kids to use blades. It worries me, so I ask the kids to use scissors *after* I start the cut for them.

Taping

I give out a yard at a time. Kids will use a whole roll if left to it. I demonstrate how much tougher and more accurate it is to use 4" strips of tape placed lengthwise. I do one side, line up for symmetry, and then tape the other.

Using Drawings as Patterns

I ask the kids to use the drawings as a pattern to cut out the fins and other parts. I find a scroll saw works great on cardboard and coroplast.

Attaching Stuff to the Bottles

Use sandpaper to scuff up wherever they want to attach things. Hot glue works well, but I find that it is used *way* too much and kids tend to burn themselves. Tape works well. The fins can also be taped on with care.

Remind the kids about a couple of things. They forget that the egg has to go in and out easily. I cut a hatch in the top bottle. Remind the students that they *must not* puncture the booster bottle at all. Usually one

team will forget this. You will also get at least one team that will forget that the booster bottle goes *top down* and they will tape the fins on upside down. Make sure they understand **symmetry** and that the rockets work really well if they are about two times the length of a bottle.

So how does this relate to the rockets? I explain that a slightly heavier rocket will go further. A *way* heavier rocket will not move at all, of course. I suggest that weight in the nose can be beneficial, but can be used *only* if it is not sharp, too heavy, or potentially dangerous. A Ziploc of sand works really well. You can tell the kids this, but they come up with great stuff on their own. One team used peanut butter, which is heavy and also worked well as a protector for the egg.

I've included a series of shots that I use to demonstrate the process to the kids. The steps show how you can add two bottles together with just a bit of duct tape. You can also use the duct tape to attach some fins. Notice also that I added water to the top (non-booster bottle).

I have kids work out plans for parachutes sometimes. They are pretty exciting for kids and sometimes work, but they need to be carefully planned. Most kids get a plastic bag, tape it to the nose, and hope it will work. It won't. If you want to explore the idea of parachutes, I suggest using plastic bags cut open and tethered properly. I've had students use a bottle cut in half, with the egg attached to the top. The bottle rests on the booster rocket but is not attached. When the rocket is accelerating, the egg bottle remains in place. When the rocket starts to slow, the air pushes the bottle off and the parachute opens.

Step 3: Day 3—Building and Newton's First Law

Tools and materials are the same as Day 2. Today, I like to start with another bit of theory. I verbally test the class to make sure they remember Newton's Second and Third Laws. Then, I introduce the First Law: "F=MA." In other words, "Stuff that is sitting there will stay that way unless something happens to it. Once things start moving, they tend to keep moving until something happens to change how it is moving."

I ask, "What would happen to the student with less mass if *nothing* was slowing them down. The students usually know that the kid would keep moving. We talk a bit about why the student stops (friction, mainly).

Now I ask them, if both the small kid and I started moving at the same speed, who would go farther? They know intuitively that I would, but why? This is where the "M" in the First Law comes in. Explain that force ("F") would increase if the mass ("M") increased. Show them simple examples on the board.

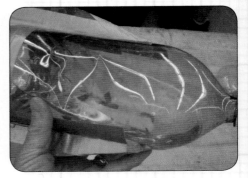

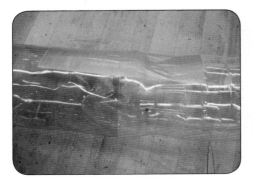

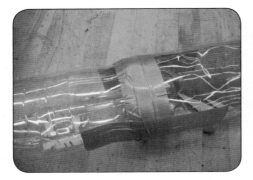

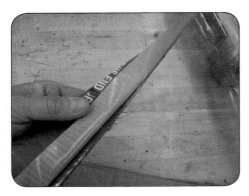

Step 4: Day 4—THE LAUNCH

I make sure the students understand the idea of adding water, as it relates to the laws of motion. It seems that the ideal amount of water is about a third of the bottle, but encourage the kids to experiment.

I bring out the Eggstronauts with much fanfare and excitement. It's fun to turn it into a goofy event. The teams submit the rocket and Eggstronaut hatch for entry. Once the water is added and the egg is in place, we launch. Make sure the kids are well back. Sometimes the rockets go sideways. The most concern for safety comes when a team builds a really accurate rocket. This means the rocket is going to come down pretty much where everyone is standing. If this happens, I get the kids to all make sure they have a back to the wall of the school. This really cuts down on the danger level. Do not let kids run after the rocket until it lands. They have a really solid punch; sometimes they leave holes in the ground.

The biggest concern for me has turned out to be the least. I was worried at first about the bottles exploding. After accidentally exploding a water bottle and a compromised pop bottle on two occasions, I can tell you the only danger is the embarrassment of needing to clean your shorts afterward. It explodes with a very impressive gunshot that scared the heck out of me both times. My guess is that, because the material is so light, it has very little momentum and doesn't cause damage other than evaporating whatever is attached to the bottle. It's pretty impressive!

I give a basic mark related to the design. It needs to look like the rocket when finished. I also give marks for accurate flight and height and a bonus mark for Eggstronaut survival.

Try this project! I've done it for years and I have twenty-year-old ex-students come back and tell me they learned more with the rockets than half their

science classes. As a shop teacher, there really is no greater compliment.

Eco Office Rocket: Build a Rocket from Trash

By: sshuggi
(http://www.instructables.com/
id/Eco-Office-Rocket-Build-a-
Rocket-from-Trash/)

Don't throw away those old papers. Turn them into a rocket! Whether you're just bored at work or want to have your own "space race" at the office while your boss is on vacation, the Eco Office Rocket is for you. It's a great way to kill time, recycle trash, and take a break from your day-to-day activities.

Step 1: Materials and Tools
Materials:

- At least four sheets of paper1 file folder or similar sturdy paper
- 1 plastic bag of any size
- 1 sheet of toilet paper
- 1 good rubber band
- 1 paperclip
- 1 pen

Tools:
- Ruler (print one)
- Scissors
- Tape

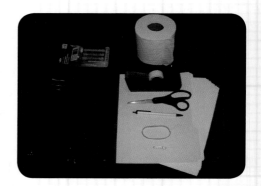

Step 2: Make the Body Tube
(Pictures relate to numbers.)

1. Determine what diameter of engine you want. As you may guess, the size and price are directly proportional. (C6-5s that I have were less than $10 for three.)
2.1. Do a simple $c = \pi d$ calculation to find out your body tube's inner diameter. (For A to C motors, use 56.55 mm.)
2.2. Make a straight line this distance, c, that is parallel from the edge of your paper.
3. Loosely roll the paper on itself with your line inside the roll.
4. Tighten up your tube such that the internal edge of the paper is lying along the line you made. Make sure the top and bottom are relatively flat.
5. Tape the tube in the middle.
6. Tape another sheet on the tube in line with the first. (Tape the top, bottom, and middle.)
7. Repeat this until you have a sturdy tube. (I used three sheets. For larger diameter motors, use more.)
8. Tape the last sheet in the middle, then the full length of the edge.

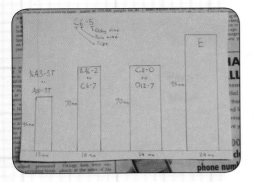

Step 3: Make the Motor Mount

(Pictures relate to numbers.)

1. Straighten out a paperclip.

2–3. Using your scissors as pliers, make a small 90° bend on one end (a little over ⅛" long).

4–5. Using the scissors again, make another 90° bend out of the other end, such that the length of your motor will fit in between. (A to C motors are 70 mm long.)

6. Make a note of where you need to insert the paperclip. You want about ¼" of the motor exposed so you can easily pull it out.)

7. Using a finger to prevent the body tube from crumpling, poke a hole through the body tube. (You may want to rough up the tip of the paperclip to make it into more of a needle.)

8. After you poke through the one side, poke through the opposite side remaining perpendicular to the body tube.

9–10. After you're through both sides, bend the remaining bit of the paperclip down.

11. Tape over the paperclip about two times.

12. Tape over the middle of the paperclip about two times. (Make sure you can still bend the bottom of the paperclip up.)

Step 4: Make the Nose Cone

(Pictures relate to numbers)

1. Disassemble your pen to just the pointy cap and the tube.
2. Cut the tube about two inches from the cap.
3. Cut long strips of paper about 1–1.5" wide.
4–5. Wrap the paper around the pen at a slight angle, starting at the cap. Loosely coil the paper at first, and then tighten to the right shape.
6–8. Add strips until it is the right diameter to fit in the body tube. (You may need to trim down the strips.)
9. Cut some half-width strip of tape. (You can easily tear them.)
10–11. Wrap them around the nose cone until you have enough to form a stop to keep the nose cone from falling into the body tube.
12–14. Wrap a long strip of tape around nose cone from the pen cap to the tape stop. (When the tape gets too high of an angle, crimp the tape and wrap over them.)
15. Gently crimp down the bottom of the nose cone so it can easily fit into the body tube.

eco office rocket: build a rocket from trash

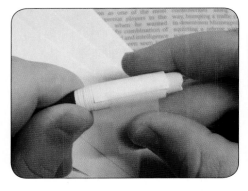

Step 5: Attaching the Nose Cone

(Pictures relate to numbers)

1. Poke a slit for your rubber band about 2" from the top. (The bottom has the motor mount.)
2. Cut your rubber band into a strip.
3. Wiggle the rubber band through your hole.

4. Cut about ½" off the end of the ink tube.

5. Knot the rubber band around the piece of the ink tube.

6. Tape the knot down into a low profile position.

7. Cut three strips of tape about 1' long.

8. Fold the tape on itself.

9. Line up the three strips and tape them onto something.

10. Braid the tape.

11. Put the right in the middle.

12. Put the left in the middle and repeat.

13–14. Tape off the ends into a tight coil.

15. Cut off the tip of the pen cap on the nose cone so the tape string can fit through.

16. Thread the string through and tie a knot to prevent it from slipping back through the hole.

17. Bend the three strips back and tape them down.

18. Tie the tape string to the rubber band.

19. Tape over the knot.

Note: The rocket tends to land on the top of the tube. It isn't going fast enough to mess it up, but add a few wraps of tape just around the top of the body tube to stiffen it up.

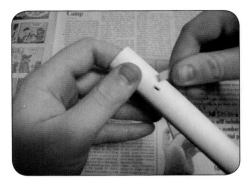

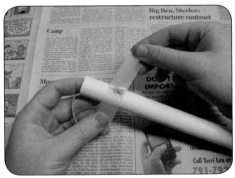

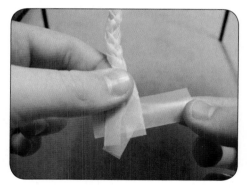

Step 6: Make the Recovery System

(Pictures relate to numbers)

1. Cut your bag into ~1" wide strips that are ~5' long. (Tie them together if you need to.)
2. Tie them onto the rubber band (maximum of two for this size motor).
3. Fold the strips.
4. Roll the strips.
5. Wad the toilet paper around the roll.
6. Insert the wad into the body tube.

Note: I chose to use streamers instead of a parachute for two reasons. One, the rocket is small and light enough that the streamers slow it well enough. Two, I am limiting myself to the tape string that is way too thick for this size body tube. If you are making a larger rocket and/or have thinner string, feel free to try and use a parachute.

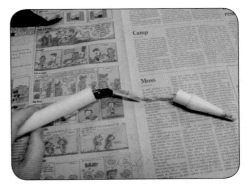

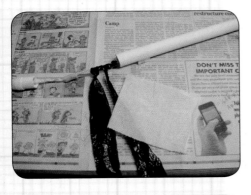

Step 7: Make the Fins

(Pictures relate to numbers)

1. Find the middle of your file folder (typically 5.75").
2. Choose a desirable fin shape. (Make the leading edge on the fold.)

3–5. Using the first fin as a guide, cut out three or four fins.

6. Cut a small slit at the top of the fins.
7. Bend out the flaps at a 90° angle to make tabs, which better stabilize the fins. (You can use a ruler/desk edge to make a clean fold.)
8. Tape down the trailing edges.

9–11. Tape the fins onto the rocket. (Avoid the motor mount; it needs to open and close.)

12. Tape the top ends of the tabs tightly.

13. Tape a couple strips around the remaining pen tube. This is called the launch lug.

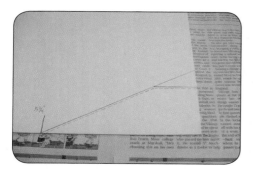

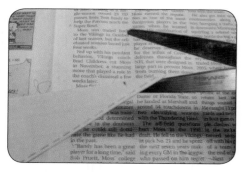

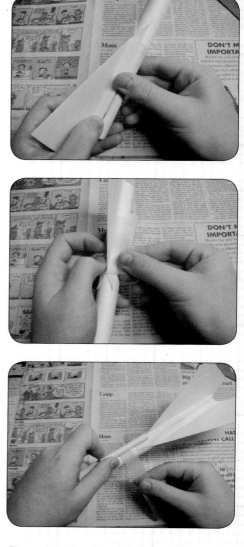

Step 8: You're Finished!

Add some color to your rocket. It'll help you see it in the sky and find it on the ground. (I went with Christmas colors because that's all I had.) Also, if your motor doesn't fit snugly in the body tube, add a wrapping of paper to snugly fit it in. You need a good seal for the ejection charge (when it blows the nose cone off and the streamers out).

I hope the build was interesting enough to get you through that boring work day. If you still have time to kill, think about adding the following things:

A payload section: All you would have to do is make a second, wider tube and a second nose cone that goes the other way.

A parachute (for wider rockets): Plastic will work, but reinforce where you attach the string. It rips easy.

Put the fins on at an angle: It makes it fly straighter, but it's tougher to attach the fins.

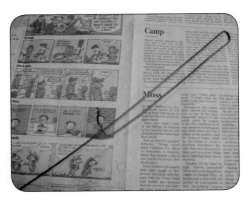

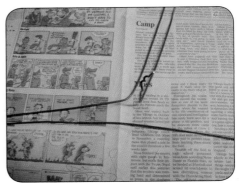

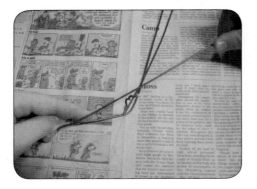

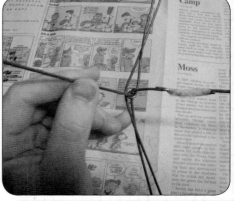

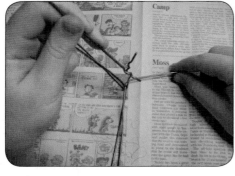

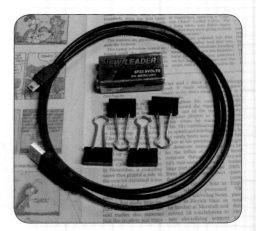

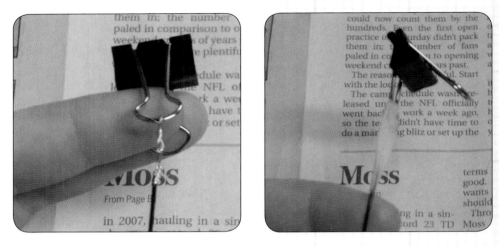

Back when I was in high school (early '90s), boredom inspired me to create a handheld rocket launcher out of miscellaneous parts I found in my dad's garage. It worked spectacularly . . . once. After that, I never got it operational again, and it eventually found its way back into the pile of parts. Recently I have been feeling exceedingly nostalgic and, for the past few years, I've felt the urge to create a new and improved version. So I now proudly present to you the Handheld Rocket Launcher Mk II.

Note: The legality of this item falls into a bit of a grey zone (similar to potato cannons). The state of Arizona is especially interesting, since model rockets are legal, but any type of firework or sparkler is not. *Do not* aim this at *any* living thing! Use common sense and safety if you choose to build/ use one of these! It is for educational and entertainment only, as it has no practical value at all. To put it bluntly, don't be an idiot with this thing. I'm not responsible for any accidents you may incur.

Step 1: Concept

The Launcher is powered by a 9-volt battery. The power has an illuminated safety switch and will not fire unless the switch is "armed." Pull the trigger and a current is passed through the copper barrel and a steel washer at the base of the barrel. If a properly constructed, missile is loaded at this time, it will complete the circuit, lighting the igniter and the missile will be launched from the barrel.

Step 2: Materials

- 1" diameter x 24" long copper pipe
- 1" threaded copper adapter
- 1" threaded PVC cap
- Piece of leather (optional)
- Wood, 2.5" × 24" × ¼"
- Wood screws #4, ⅝"
- #12, 2" machine bolt w/ nut (not shown)
- 18-gauge speaker wire (I also used other smaller wires as well)
- Insulated ring terminal (two different sizes)
- 2 fender washers, ⅛" × ¾"
- Momentary contact push button
- Illuminated toggle switch
- 9-volt clip
- 1" insulated clamps
- Steel rivet, ⅛" diameter x ½" grip

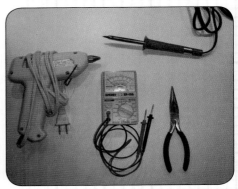

Step 3: Tools

- Drill
- Jigsaw
- Miscellaneous drill bits (including ½" and 1") (not shown)
- Screwdriver
- Dremel (equired for virtually *every* project)
- Needle-nose pliers
- Wire strippers
- Torch
- Rivet tool (What's the proper name for this?)
- Soldering iron (optional but recommended)
- Ohmmeter (optional but recommended)
- Hot glue gun (optional but recommended)

Step 4: Copper Work

Solder the copper fitting to the pipe. It's recommended to coat the end of the pipe and the inside of the fitting with flux prior to soldering. It helps the solder flow into the joint. Using the torch, heat the fitting (not the pipe itself). Once hot enough, the solder will melt and be sucked into the joint. Wipe it down with a rag and let it cool.

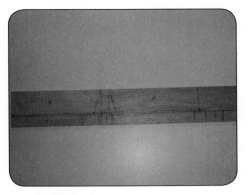

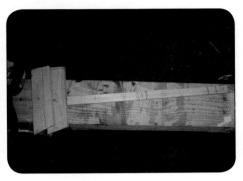

Step 5: Wood Cutting

Using the supplied schematic at the end of this Instructable, mark out the pieces onto the wood as shown. Start by cutting the strip with B, C, and D off. I used a jigsaw, but a table saw would have been much better for this step. Cut out pieces A and B next. To create a perfect curved end to B and C, clamp them to a working surface, and then drill out the circle using a 1" bit. Do not drill the holes for the buttons yet!

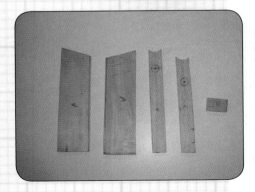

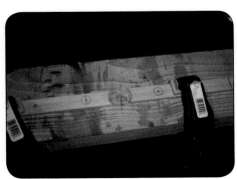

Step 6: Handle Construction

Mark out the locations of the button holes and ends on the wood pieces. You will need these lines to locate the holes for the screws. Be sure to stagger the holes in such a way that ensures they don't enter any of the button holes, and they won't hit each other. I went a bit overboard with the holes. You'll see in photos of the final product that I didn't need this many. Use your own discretion on this step.

Since the heads of the screws have a taper on them, we'll need to countersink the holes a bit. If we don't, there is a good chance the screws will split the wood. I used a small boring bit on the Dremel to create the countersinks.

Assemble the handle. Be sure to use pilot holes for the screws so that the wood does not split! Drill the button holes using a ½" bit, keeping them as centered as possible. I decided on a whim to stain the handle. Definitely not required but adds to the "cool factor" (an important quality in all of my instructables).

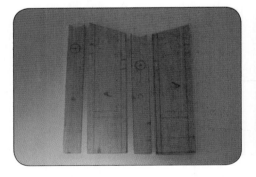

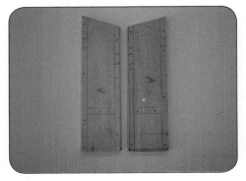

Step 7: Handle Attachment

For me, this was the most difficult part of the build. Take your time on this step. Take the two 1" clamps, and if yours are insulated, remove the insulation. Bend them so both legs are at equal lengths. Next, position them over the barrel and onto the handle in such a way that the bracket will hold the handle flush. Drill a $7/32$" hole through the handle. It will have to be located so as to miss both switches. On my prototype it was a little bit loose, and I had to resort to using the hot glue gun to keep the handle from slipping around on the barrel.

Step 8: Ignition System

Open up the handle and install the electronics per the attached schematic. Make sure the threads on your buttons are long enough to penetrate the wood. I almost had to countersink my trigger! When you have it put together, pull the speaker wire almost all of the way apart. Cut the positive lead to just a few inches long and attach a ring terminal large enough to go over the #12 bolt. The negative lead should be about 16" long. Once wired up, it is recommended you test the system using your ohmmeter. Set it to 10V DC test and connect it to the end terminals. You need to verify there is *only* a charge when both the safety switch is on *and* the trigger is pushed. This is a very important step. You do not want this thing firing unexpectedly. The safety switch should illuminate when it's "armed."

To eliminate the possibility of a short, I filled the button terminals with hot glue. Next, scuff up the top of the battery clip and, using wood glue, attach it to piece D. I used cellophane tape to secure it in place while the glue dried.

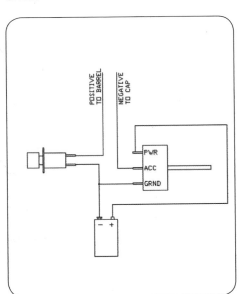

205

and taping it to the end of the barrel. Start each port with an ⅛" hole, and then enlarge to a ³⁄₁₆" bit. Do not apply too much pressure with the drill or you could deform the barrel.

After the holes are drilled, take your Dremel or a file, and spend the time to make the inside of the barrel smooth again. If it's not smooth enough the fins of the missile might get caught. Not pretty.

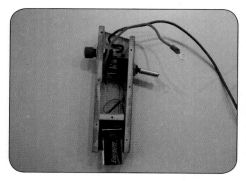

Step 9: Barrel Porting

I chose to "port" the barrel for a couple of reasons. First it (hypothetically) will reduce turbulence for the missile by allowing the gases to escape from the sides of the barrel instead of competing for room at the mouth of the barrel. Other than that, it looks rather cool, and I'm anticipating short flames/smoke shooting from them ("cool factor").

Begin by printing the template provided at the end of this Instructable

Step 10: Handle Attachment

With the handle reassembled, cut a small notch in the arch above the safety switch with your Dremel. Lay the wires in this notch and then attach the handle to the barrel with your 1" clamps and bolt. Slip the positive lead ring terminal over the bolt. Wrap the negative lead around the barrel a few times and cut to the desired length. Attach the smaller ring terminal to the negative lead.

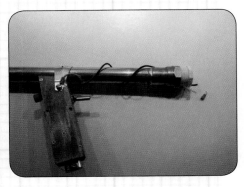

Step 11: End Cap Construction and Testing

Drill a ⅛" hole in the cap. Widen it slightly. Starting from the outside, the rivet should pass through the ring terminal, a washer, a piece of card stock (more on that in a second), through the cap, and then secure the second washer inside the cap.

The card stock was a good idea that didn't work well at all. I wanted the ring terminal to be able to spin on the rivet.

I had planned on ripping the card stock out but the rivet gripped too hard and I never got it out. Perhaps if I had put the card stock on the other side of the washer it would have worked better.

After this step is complete, get out your ohmmeter again. Set it to 10V DC and touch the positive probe to the barrel and the negative to the inside washer on the PVC cap. Verify that you are getting 9-volts when the trigger is pulled.

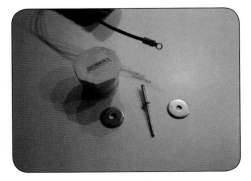

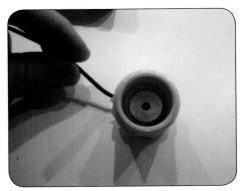

207

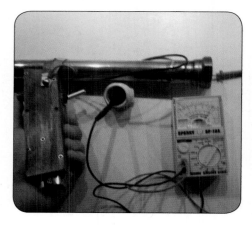

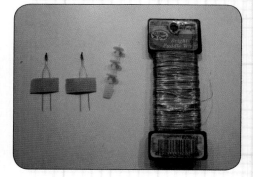

Step 12: Missile Construction

Materials needed:

- Pack of rocket engines (with igniters and plugs)
- Printed templates from the end of this Instructable
- Thin conductive tying wire

Any standard size rocket engine will work. I had some B4-4s lying around that I used. The ideal rocket would be a C engine used for glider rockets. These have no ejection charge, so they have a better power to weight ratio.

Cut out the fins and nosecone templates. Bend the fins in a series of peaks and valleys as shown. Wrap and glue around the top of the rocket engine. These cannot go at the bottom of the rocket or it will not sit properly inside the PVC cap. Next, cut out and glue the nosecones on as shown.

Install the igniter as you normally would using the plastic plug. Remove the tape holding the leads together. Bend one lead up the side of the rocket. Twist the other lead into a coil-spring. These leads *must not touch* or it will not fire. Cut a piece of tying wire and loop it against the straight lead, securing it in place with a small piece of tape. This tying wire must bend outward as shown to ensure it makes contact with the copper barrel.

Step 13: Launch Aftermath

It works, but the rockets weren't nearly as stable as I had hoped. Perhaps using different strength engines would help, or creating a longer missile by taping a used engine to the front of a fresh engine. Weighting the nose cone could also be beneficial.

The escaping gases actually stung my hand a little bit.

The rocket has to be cleaned out at least a little between shots. If there is too much residue in the barrel, the ignition wires can't pick up the current.

handheld rocket launcher!

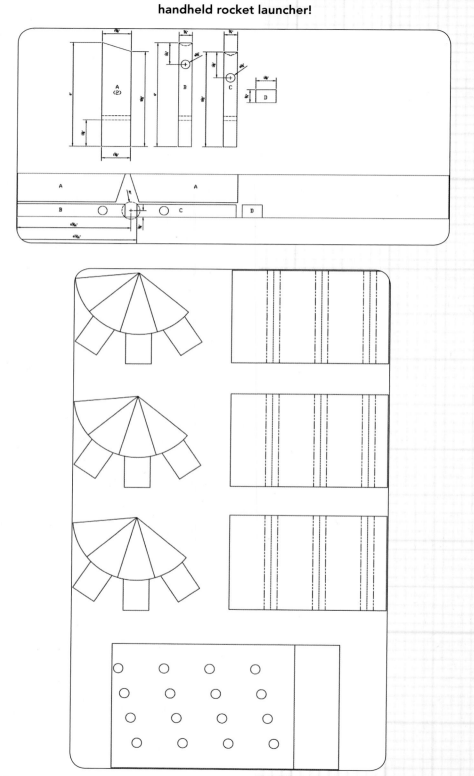

PVC paper rocket launcher designs are a dime-a-dozen. So why another one? Because I've tried many other designs found on Google and YouTube, and none of them are fairly easy to build, perform spectacularly, or are easy for kids to operate. I have finally come up with a design that fulfills all the criteria for an amazing rocket launcher, after conducting the paper rocket project with my engineering class countless times.

This Instructable also outlines how to make a high-performing rocket, which is just as important as having a great launcher. The students in my engineering class have made rockets that can fly over 100 yards from this launcher—it's rather mind-blowing to witness.

Step 1: Make the Launcher

I work with elementary-school aged children, so making the launcher is something I do as part of my prep. Older kids (with a generous budget) can try to design their own launcher. View the last step for a complete list of materials.

This launcher works up to 60 PSI. You can wire in a second 9-volt battery to get the launcher up to 100 PSI. Sixty PSI is enough to achieve spectacular results. Pressures above that dramatically increase the risk of exploding the rocket, and, in my experience, most student-built rockets cannot withstand the speeds produced by more than 70 PSI.

By the way, you might want to protect your work surface a bit better than I did.

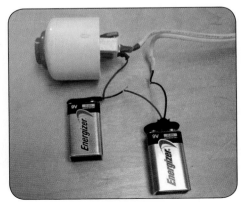

Step 2: Make the Rocket

- Card stock
- Tape
- Scissors

It's easy to build a rocket that can reach a distance of 50'. However, making an ultra-high-performing rocket is actually quite challenging, because all aspects need to be designed to near perfection. At high speeds, tiny imperfections are quickly blown out of proportion because the forces acting upon the rocket are intensified. For example, a nose cone that leans slightly to one side may not significantly influence the rocket's performance at 40 PSI. However, at 60 PSI, that nose cone may create an imbalance of friction created by the air rushing by, causing the rocket to turn sharply and tumble to the ground.

For this reason, take your time while creating and attaching each part of the rocket. And with that in mind, here's how to make a high-performing rocket

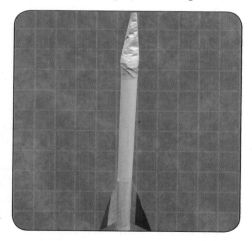

Step 3: The Lesson (for Teachers)

Learning Objective

- Fundamental concepts in aerodynamics such as stability, drag, and propulsion are experientially explored and applied as students build and test their rockets. The comprehension of these concepts is further strengthened as students redesign and retest their rockets while observing the differences in performance.
- Students will acknowledge the value of teamwork as they work in pairs to design and build their rocket.
- Students who choose to work individually will quickly observe the value of teamwork during certain steps.
- Basic rocket anatomy vocabulary (fuselage, fins, and nose cone) will be understood and utilized during the teacher's lecture and during rocket construction.
- Fine motor skills are developed during rocket construction.
- Optional: Students will experientially comprehend the values of different materials as they apply their material choices to their rocket design, as well as by observing the performance of different material combinations.

Lesson Plan

I usually start by explaining how the launcher works because it catches the students' attention right away. I just explain the basics: The chamber is filled with air, creating high air pressure, and when the button is pressed, the air is allowed to escape through the launch tube, which provides propulsion to the rockets.

Next, I show the class how to build a rocket from start to finish. I usually work a little fast and imprecisely since I'm just outlining the steps, so be sure to encourage them to take their time and build with precision. As I build the rocket, I explain the important aspects of each part:

The fuselage must fit the ½" PVC perfectly. If it is too tight, it will not fit, or it will explode upon launch. If it's too loose, propulsion (pressurized air) will escape out from the bottom of the rocket. The fuselage should slide onto the launch tube with little wiggle room.

The fins provide stability for the rocket—this is enough explanation for younger students. Older students may benefit from knowing this: When a rocket is pushed off course by a gust of wind, the angle of attack (direction the air is moving) relative to the fins changes, which causes the fins to generate a small amount of lift. The lift immediately forces the rocket to return to its original trajectory, which also restores the angle of attack to 0, thus stabilizing the rocket. If the fins are too large or not straight, it may generate too much lift and cause the rocket to turn during flight. If a rocket begins to turn because of the fins, the center of pressure (the point at which all forces are acting upon the rocket, including momentum and lift) surpasses the center of gravity, meaning the rocket will try to turn around, causing it to tumble out of control. Basically, make your fins precisely and tape them on straight!

The nose cone reduces drag (air pushing against all sides of the rocket) by offering minimum aerodynamic resistance. In other words, the nosecone helps the rocket "push" its way through the air without allowing the air to push back against the tip of the rocket, instead flowing smoothly around it. Demonstrate how to build the nose cone a few times since it can be challenging. The nose cone can be difficult for young students to build, so an alternative (though less effective) design is to simply pinch the end of the rocket and close it with tape. Be sure to tell the students to secure their nose cone extremely well because the air pressure can blow the cone off of the rocket.

Inspect each part of the rocket for straightness and secure placement.

I also encourage the students to work in pairs for this project for two reasons. Firstly, it is simply easier to construct a rocket if one person holds the parts in position while the other secures it with tape; secondly, flaws in the rocket design are more easily identified and resolved when two people are examining the design and expressing their thoughts and ideas.

Remember, the objective is to allow students to explore and comprehend aerospace ideas experientially, so allow them to experiment with different rocket lengths, nose cone and fin shapes, number of fins, etc. It's okay if students cannot give you a textbook definition of ideas like drag and trajectory at the end of class. As long as they are engaged with the activity, they will learn these things effortlessly.

Alternative Ideas

You can offer a myriad of materials for the students to explore and build with, which adds a new dimension to the project. Experimenting with different materials can add longevity to the lesson.

Step 4: Safety, Tips, and Troubleshooting

Follow these safety precautions regardless of whether the chamber is pressurized or loaded with a rocket.

- Never allow students to use the launcher unsupervised. Disable the launcher by removing the battery (or pump or launch tube) if you have to leave the launcher unsupervised.
- Never allow anyone to put their face near the launch tube. Air expelled from the tube, if forced into someone's nose or mouth, is powerful enough to cause the lungs to rupture. This is very serious. Tell your students about this and they will be frightened enough to never

get near the tip of the launch tube.

- Never stand directly in front of the launcher, even if a rocket is not loaded. At point blank, a rocket shot from the launcher can cause serious injury.
- The student holding the button should keep his/her trigger finger off of the button until the final countdown is initiated. The button is sensitive and can easily misfire.
- Use a bright rope to define a safety zone that the students may never cross, even while loading their rocket.
- Have a countdown before each launch as a way to alert people in the area (and to make each launch more exciting!).

Common Design Flaws

- Fins that are not attached straight, or if the leading tip of the fin is not secured, will cause the rocket to tumble at high speeds.
- Fins that are too big create too much lift and/or drag.
- Fins that are too small may not provide enough stability.
- Fins that extend too far from the fuselage are prone to wobbling in the wind, causing instability.
- Nose cones that are not secured well enough will explode off of the rocket.

Tips and Troubleshooting

Rockets tend to explode at pressures above 60 PSI. If you choose to mod the button with a second 9-volt battery, have the students tape up every seam many times over.

Inspect the rocket before each flight and use your hands to straighten out the fins and nose cone, which will inevitably become bent over time.

I usually refrain from interfering with students' designs. However, if a student has created a poorly built fuselage I will step in and help them. Making a new fuselage after attaching everything else can be a hassle.

Young students (grades three and below) may have a hard time rolling a tube of card stock, so I usually do that step as part of my prep.

If you don't have access to a huge open space, you can set up targets like stacked cardboard boxes and aim for those. Be extra cautious here.

When storing the launcher, remove the 9-volt battery, or at least make sure the button is uncompressed, or else the battery will quickly drain.

Step 5: Materials List

Here's the complete list of materials and tools for the launcher and paper rockets.

Tools for the air pressure chamber

- Sandpaper
- PVC cutting tool
- Drill
- Mallet
- Pipe wrench
- Latex gloves

Materials for the air pressure chamber

- PVC primer
- PVC solvent weld (aka PVC cement)
- KwikPlastic (or similar)
- Tire valve
- 2 6" sections of 2-inch PVC

- 2 2" slip fit end cap
- 2" slip fit T-joints
- 2" to 1" slip fit reducer
- 2" section of 1" PVC
- 2 1" threaded male adapter
- 1" to ½" slip fit reducer
- 24" piece of ½" PVC with tapered end
- Modified valve and replacement launch handle from ItsaBlast.com
- Bicycle pump with PSI gauge

For the base
- 12" cable ties
- 2 PVC elbow joints
- 2 12" piece of PVC with two holes drilled about 4" apart
- 8" piece of PVC

For paper rockets
- Card stock
- Masking tape
- Scissors

The total cost is about $70, excluding all tools and solvent weld. In my line of work, it is well worth the initial investment because the paper rocket activity is very cheap—less than $0.15 per student.

Pocket Rocket Launcher

By: zjharva
(http://www.instructables.com/
id/Pocket-Rocket-Launcher/)

This is a real rocket launcher that fits in your pocket. It is easy and cheap!

Step 1: Parts and Tools

Almost all of these can be bought at Radioshack.

Materials
- Altoids' tin
- DPDT Heavy Duty Rocker Switch
- Mini SPST Momentary Push Button Switch
- Red LED with holder And built-in resistor
- 9-volt battery snap
- 9-volt battery
- 9/16" wide copper tubing (can be found at Radioshack)
- Alligator clip
- Test leads
- Wire A10-3T or A10-PT rocket engines (available at Hobbytown)

Tools
- Wire strippers
- Pliers
- Metal snippers
- Pocket knife
- Soldering iron
- Hot glue gun
- Pipe cutter
- Drill
- Large drill bits
- Small drill bit
- Block of wood
- Clamp

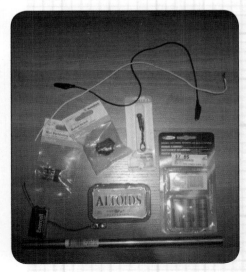

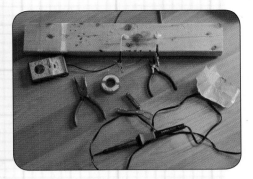

Step 2: Getting the Tin Ready

This step involves creating holes for the rocket and switches to go through.

Parts and Tools

- Altoids' tin
- Pliers
- Metal snippers
- Drill
- Large drill bits
- A small drill bit
- Round file
- Clamp
- Wood block

Bend the metal tabs holding the lid on back. Remove the lid. Bend one tab so that there is no hole in the tin. Then, bend one tab so it is flat against the tin (picture 1). Cut off the bottom metal on one of the holes on the lid (picture 2). Mark the size of the holes for the switch and tubing. Put a block of wood in the tin and clamp it down. This makes the tin not bend. Drill them out. If the holes aren't big enough, file them out (picture 3, 4, 5, and 6). Drill a hole in the back for the LED using previous techniques (picture 7). Shave off some of the screw on ring of the rocker switch (picture 8). Cut an approximately 3" piece of pipe. If the pipe cutter made an indent on the pipe, file it out (pictures 9 and 10). Check and see if everything fits (picture 11).

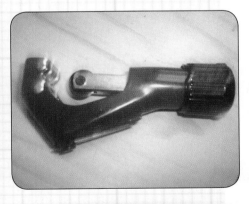

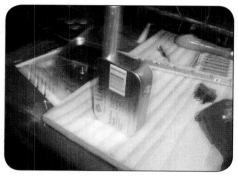

together. Be sure to slip on shrink wrap before you solder it. Then shrink the shrink wrap (pictures 1 and 2). Solder the red wire from the battery snap to one of the tabs on it. Be sure to shrink wrap it. Then, solder a short piece of wire to the other tab (pictures 3, 4, and 5). Solder the red wire from the LED, a short piece of wire, and the wire from the rocker switch together. Shrink wrap it all with the short piece of wire sticking out back towards the switch (picture 6; disregard the color of the wire, it was just some salvaged wire). Solder the short piece of wire to one of the tabs on the momentary switch, and shrink wrap it. Solder the other alligator clip to the other tab of the momentary switch and shrink wrap it (pictures 7 and 8). When you turn the rocker switch on, the back LED should light up. If the alligator clips are touching and you press the momentary switch, the LED should go out (picture 9).

Step 3: Solder It

This is the step when you solder the switches.

Parts and Tools

- Rocker switch
- Push momentary switch
- LED
- 9-volt battery snap
- Soldering iron
- Solder
- Wire
- Wire stripper

Cut the alligator clips in half so you have two alligator clips with wires. Solder the battery snap's black wire, the LED's black wire, and one alligator clip

Step 4: Finishing Touches

For the finishing touches you need:

- Hot glue gun
- Hot glue sticks
- Soda can
- Scissors
- Metal snips
- Electrical tape (optional)
- Scissors

Measure and cut a piece of soda can metal the length and height of the tin, with a notch big enough for the wires

to go through. Cover with tape for a "stealthy" look. This is the blast shield (picture 1). Glue all of the solder points and wires down, except for the alligator clips and the battery snap. Also, glue the blast shield and launch tube (picture 2). Cut out a slot on top for the rocker switch so you can close it all the way (pictures 3 and 4).

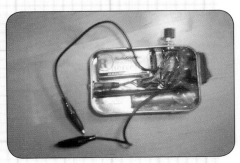

Step 5: Launching!

This is what you need to launch it:

- The assembled launcher
- Rocket motor
- Rocket igniter
- Ignitor plug
- Gloves
- Common sense

Insert the igniter, plug into the rocket, and slide down the tube. Connect the alligator clips. Put on your gloves and turn on the rocker switch. Make sure the LED comes on (picture 1). Use your brain and common sense. Point away from people, pets, and flammable things. Press the button. After a little delay and a puff of smoke, off it goes (picture 2)!

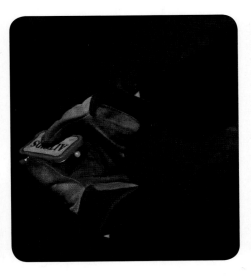

Rocket-Powered Matchbox Cars— Extreme!

By: Kipkay
(http://www.instructables.
com/id/New-Rocket-Powered-
Matchbox-Cars!---Extreme!/)

First of all, my inspiration for this project came from zjharva. This is a new version of Rocket-Powered Matchbox cars. Now you see what they really do on rocket power! I used Hot Wheels cars, but I felt they really needed to be called Matchbox because of what were about to do to them!

Step 1: What You Need

First of all, you will need a package of Estes A10-PT model rocket engines. You can find these at most Walmart stores, hobby shops, or other stores that carry model rockets.

Step 2: You Also Need

Something to attach the "engines" to the cars. I used 32-gauge wire that you can wrap around the vehicle and secure the engine safely during ignition.

Step 3: And . . .

You need something to guide the car on its track. Without this, the rocket shoots the car and rolls it, flipping and tumbling across the track. I used a coffee stirrer and, after cutting a small groove in the bottom of the car, cut it to size and glued it in place. This is the perfect diameter for the string that the car rides on.

Step 4: The Controller

I picked up an Estes Race Controller that runs on four AA batteries and has a long enough wire with alligator clips at the end. These will attach to the rocket igniters and fire the rocket!

Step 5: Final Test Results!

This was wicked fun! We brought them to a tennis court, which was the perfect flat surface, and tested them out.

Projects to Get You
Off the Grid

- -

Backyard Chicken Coop

By robbtoberfest
(www.instructables.com/id/
Backyard-Chicken-Coop/)

I made this little chicken barn a few years ago to house three to five laying hens in my back yard. I'm in town and had to design a "pretty" one to keep people from having a chicken coup. This one was inspired by some Kansas barns I've seen. The total cost was about $40 when fully completed. Chicken wire, some 2 × 4s, and damaged siding were the costs. Damaged siding is half price at my local lumber store. Other things I used were scrap wood from old bathroom cabinets, leftover hardware, paint, and wood from house projects, plus a lot of scraps and hardware from a condemned house down the street (I got permission to take things before they bulldozed it). Shingles were given to me by my neighbor, leftover from roofing his garage. There are some basic rules for designing and running a good healthy chicken shack:

1. Adequate floor space per bird.
2. Dry with good ventilation.
3. Temperature control.
4. Predator protection.
5. Keep it clean+fresh water/ food=happy and healthy birds.

Many towns actually allow up to five chickens but no roosters. Check local rules on this if you plan to build. If you do get chickens in town, be courteous to the non-chicken majority so the rest of the city chicken people don't get punished through politics and zoning. I submitted pictures of this coop to someone who was working on a coops book a while ago and they included a picture of it in *Chicken Coops, 45 Building Plans for Housing Your Flock*, by Judy Pangman. Sources for my chicken knowledge: *Building Chicken Coops* by Gail Damerow; The City Chicken; Raising Backyard Chickens; Feathersite; and the

Poultry Page. I recently posted another coop, a chicken outhouse with a beer can roof at diylife.com.

Step 1: Floor Space, Framing, and Nest Boxes

My floor space includes the exterior run. I knew I wanted three heavy egg layers, so from the charts I used 10 square feet per bird rule. There are different suggestions in different books/ guides; there is a pretty good chart at Virginia Cooperative Extension. I built this 18" off the ground to create a shady part of the pen underneath the coop. The floor is 2 × 4s framed like a little porch 3 feet by 4 feet sitting on 4 × 4s attached with many 3" screws. The walls are just under 4' tall and I used 3" screws to put together the 2 × 4s. Four-foot walls are a good dimension because siding and plywood come in 4' × 8' sheets. I framed in the next boxes here. I think a rule is one box per three to five laying birds. They like dark, comfy places to lay. Making the boxes the size of a 12" dustpan works great when cleaning the coop. Many books suggest elevated boxes, but these floor boxes have worked great for three years now. Avoid treated lumber inside the coop or where they perch; the toxic stuff can affect the birds (i.e. sickness/death).

Step 2: Roof

I don't have many step-by-step pics for this so you'll have to use your skills to fill in the gaps. I cut 2 × 4s with angles to make three sets of rafters and attached them with 3" screws. I screwed down some old cabinet wood across the rafters to make the roof, leaving a little 4" hole near the center peak for a cupola. Then I shingled the roof leaving the center peak hole open. The cupola is made like a little bird house that sits over the vent hole. Use a hole saw to make holes in its sides and staple window screen on the inside to keep out the critters. Attach it with 3" screws. This helps meet rule #2: Dry with good ventilation.

Step 3: Walls

Cut the siding to fit the framing and attach it with nails. Use a jigsaw to cut out doors and other openings; save the cutouts for building the doors. Keep the following in mind while designing walls: Make openings for windows; this is important for summer heat control. Build walls tight to keep out wind and drafts; this is important for winter cold control. This is a standard chicken coop rule: Have good ventilation but no drafts.

Step 4: Doors

A main door for you to access the coop and a small chicken door are the only doors really needed. But I added cabinet doors, a nest box door, chicken door and a main door on this thing. The hinges I used were from old bath and kitchen cabinets. The main door was made with old porch flooring. Boards were attached diagonally to the siding cutout with nails; then I used the jigsaw to clean it up around the outside. This made the door look more old fashioned. The nails will stick out the back side; bend them over or cut them and grind the stubs smooth. The other doors were made directly from the siding material and some trim wood. I just attached hinges and handles with some trim around the edges. The trim is important to close the gap where the saw cut the siding. I added some plastic near the top to shed rain over the cabinet doors.

Step 5: Finishing Touches

Add the roost perch for night time. Make a perch out of a 2 × 4 with the edges rounded a bit. Under the perch make a place for the droppings to gather. This roost area is usually the only place inside of the coop where the droppings are, which makes cleaning easy. (Don't use treated wood!) When I finished the coop, it ended up being very heavy, so I attached some boards to the bottom and used a hand truck to wheel it (with help) to its home location. The run/pen can be made easily with 2 × 2s and 2 × 4s as seen in the pic below. I enclosed the top of the run to keep the hawks out. I later added a matching run on the opposite side when I added some more hens.

Step 6: Extra Notes

I've changed the coop a little over the years to allow for more birds. I've removed the storage area and added a roost in its place. Also, I've removed the small pen and made a large run for the birdies.

Small Chicken Tractor for the City Dweller

By Jrossetti

In this Instructable, I'll outline the requirements for a small chicken tractor for the backyard chicken enthusiast, such as myself, and describe the process of building it. After seeing a lot of chicken tractors on the internet for outrageous prices, I decided it'd be better for me to build a cheaper one myself that fit my needs a bit better. I'll show you how I did it and give some pointers on making your own design.

For those of you who don't know what a chicken tractor is, it's essentially a chicken coop that can be moved around. Some of the main purposes for a mobile chicken coop are to allow the chickens to fertilize the grass (though this isn't pretty at all), eat the grass (keeping it trim if done right), and eat bugs and weeds, and so it is easy to hide when your parents come to visit. There's other benefits too, though I'm not saying a coop is *not* the way to go (my city actually has an ordinance stating any permanent chicken coop must be forty feet away from any human house, so a tractor is a nice, efficient way to bypass that ordinance).

A lot of what went into my design is the direct result of trial and error and the input of the very knowledgeable people over at www.backyardchickens.com.

So let's begin.

I started the project with the following goals:

- Small enough to be moved by hand around my property
- Big enough to comfortably house one to four chickens
- General protection from the elements (sun, wind, rain, etc)

233

- Protection from predators
- Easy access to the things I need to access

And of course, the following elements were required:

- henhouse (where the chickens could sleep at night) with proper ventilation
- nesting box (where they lay eggs)
- covered run area (chickens don't like sun tanning, or standing in the rain)
- food and water support for at least one day

So moving on to the first step we'll take a look at the design.

Step 1: My Tractor Design

From the intro, we have a general list of what we need to include in the design to make it successful. This list is the absolute bare minimum I would suggest any chicken tractor or even a chicken coop should include to make the upkeep easy for you and reduce worry.

Size and Construction

I wanted a tractor big enough for my chickens. I started out with three chickens but may have as many as four or five. Most sources on the Internet agree that chickens need a minimum of 1 square foot of indoor space and 2 square feet of outdoor space to live, and, of course, any more than that and they're even happier. So based on that math, I'd need a henhouse size no smaller than 4 square feet, and a run no smaller than 8 square feet. I can do that!

I ended up on dimensions of 3 feet wide, 7 feet long, and about 4 feet tall at the highest point. That is about 21 square feet of run space, and the henhouse is 9 square feet (3' by 3') and is about 3 feet tall at the highest point.

Most of the frame will be made using 2" by 2" pine, the base frame from 2 × 4s, and the rest with whatever is cheapest.

Protection from the Elements

Now, with that list in hand, my next consideration is the environment the tractor will be in. In my case, it's all level ground with a mix of bare ground (the garden area), grass (lawn area), and concrete (driveway and side yard). I also have fruit trees and shade trees. The weather is hot and dry in the summer and snowy in the winter, so we need to take all of that into consideration in designing the tractor.

So, it's pretty much a given that with all the different types of ground the tractor can travel on, we'll need wheels. A sled-type of setup won't work too well.

Chickens don't do too well in the sun, so they'll need shade. They'll get that with the trees in parts of the property, but not all, so I need to design a roof that will cover the run area of the tractor. And since it snows in the winter, it's probably a good idea to slant the roof to shed the snow (and rain in the spring time).

So I decided a roof slanted towards one end, made from PVC roofing, is probably the cheapest and easiest solution.

The base of the tractor is made with redwood, which is more water resistant than pine or normal construction materials. Plus, I didn't want to use any chemically-treated woods, as if the chickens peck at it they might get sick.

Protection from Predators

I want it to be heavy enough that it can't be moved by any 'normal' predator (dogs, cats, raccoons, etc). But I also want it light enough to move by hand. I also want it to be able to repel entry by most predators, so I won't be using chicken wire! I don't want any opening larger than about 1 square inch (even though I'm sure mice can get in that anyway, I just don't want anything larger squeezing in).

I will be using 1/2" hardware cloth for the sides, screwed down with big screws and washers, so it can't be pulled out easily. Any doors will be secured with bolts or safety hooks, so most predators won't be able to get in.

Ventilation

The most important part of the henhouse is ventilation. There's plenty of material out there on the net describing the dangers of improper ventilation in a henhouse and what you can do to mitigate those dangers. I am of the opinion that more is better, so I designed it with that in mind.

The whole inside wall is open to the outside, with a removable panel that covers the lower portion in the winter. The upper back of the henhouse is a hinged vent panel, so I can open it wide in the summer and close it more in the winter.

Easy Access

I want to be able to easily access the food, water, and nesting box in order to top off the food and water and take eggs. Also, I want to be able to easily get into the henhouse for cleaning, and the run area for the same reason. I additionally want to be able to open and close the henhouse door from the outside.

So I've kind of integrated the waterer and feeder into the design since I don't have a lot of space to work with. We'll take a look at those in the next couple of steps.

The Decision

So, with all of this in mind, I will construct the tractor using wood, hardware, cloth, some PVC roofing and whatever other bits and bobs I find along the way that I need. The design went through a few different revisions, but here's a couple of pictures of what the final design looks like.

I have the final plan available in Google Sketchup format for those wanting exact dimensions. You'll find it on step 5 of this Instructable.

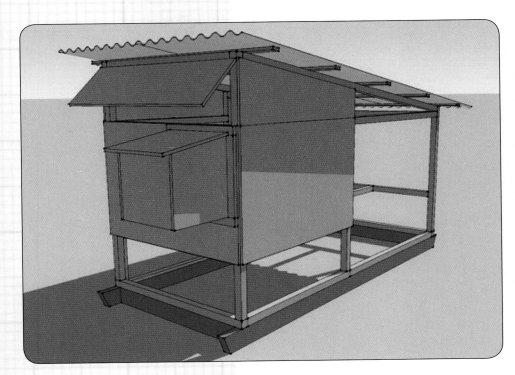

Step 2: The Waterer

Normally, a watering system for chickens consists of a hanging waterer. They usually take up a lot of space and are messy because the chickens can get water everywhere. I didn't want that and don't have a lot of space to waste on it, so I opted for a nipple system, like what's used in the bigger chicken factories. The nipple waterer is very efficient, gravity fed because it relies on very little pressure, and is actually pretty easy and cheap to implement.

I got my nipples from TekSupply. They also have a version that is a push-in type. These work better for how I used them, but this is a DIY-as-you-go type of project so you might have better luck with the others. In any case, I bought a handful of each just in case.

The nipples are plugged into 3/8" ID Vinyl tubing, which is plugged into a 2-gallon bucket that sits on a little shelf up in the side of the henhouse. I have two of them in this setup: one inside the henhouse and one outside down in the run area. The TekSupply page for the nipples say they don't require a drip cup, and, for the most part, that's true; but keep in mind that most chickens are partially psychotic and I've seen them get water all over the place even with these little things. So you may want to consider getting a drip cup if yours are consistently messy.

One other thing to keep in mind is that you want at least 12 inches of height between the nipple and the bottom of the water supply, so you can get at least a couple psi to keep the nipple from dripping.

The bucket is more or less in place. I can easily remove it should the need arise. I just need to detach the tubing from the bucket when I do. It's easily filled using a plant watering can with a long spout; mine holds enough to fill it half way. Win!

Winter Problems

When I filled it with water to test it in the winter, I noticed it'd freeze up. I solved this by putting a 50 watt aquarium heater into the bucket, and kept the nipples from freezing by placing the inside nipple immediately next to the small radiant heater I'm already using to add a little warmth for the chickens. You'll see what I'm talking about in a photo attached to the last step.

The outside nipple I keep from freezing using a small 35 watt halogen reflector bulb. It keeps it warm enough to do the job and sheds a little light so the chickens can see what they're doing, if that's even remotely important.

of elbows, and strapped it onto the side of the henhouse, with the working end sticking through the hardware cloth. The chickens dig it. It's not quite big enough that more than one can eat at a time, but they're generally amiable and will wait—or will shove somebody aside so they can get to it.

I spray-painted it to add some UV protection because ABS doesn't play very well with sunlight.

I put cheap caps on the ends to keep bugs out while I was building it. The lower cap I'll probably stick back on whenever I'm moving the tractor to keep feed from going everywhere and whenever I fill it. The upper cap I keep on all the time, to keep the mice out.

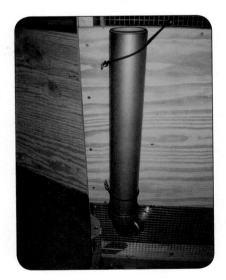

Step 3: The Feeder

I also didn't feel like I had a lot of room to put in a regular feeder, so I built my own. I built it using black ABS pipe. I obtained a 2' length of 3" pipe, plugged it into a reducer with a couple

Step 4: Construction

I constructed the whole frame using standard 2 × 2s, 2 × 4s, and gold screws. I used some brackets and doodads where I thought it would help with stability.

Check out the pictures to see how it all went together.

After I got the basic frame put together, I added the henhouse floor, worked on the nesting box, and got the henhouse all put together before adding the hardware cloth/mesh sides. You'll notice I used some plastic mesh on the top of the run area and henhouse both; it's much lighter than the steel stuff, and since the chickens are unlikely to ever come in contact with it, it doesn't need to be as durable. I fastened it in the same way, though, with big screws and washers for support.

The henhouse door has a spring on the back side to keep it closed when it's supposed to be. It opens by pulling on that chain, and is kept open with a long bolt that's slid into the two eye bolts, one on the door and one on the frame. The same eye bolt is used to "lock" the door shut at night. Yes, there is space in the door pieces, mostly for ventilation, but also because it looks cool.

The upper rear vent window uses clear PVC roofing. That's for light inside the henhouse, but also because I had some spare clear PVC leftover from another project and this was a perfect fit. I can look into the henhouse and see what the girls are up to with disturbing them too much.

Speaking of PVC roofing—I attached the PVC roof using small screws and "sealing washers." These are washers with a rubber gasket on one side. Once I got it all fastened down, I tested it out with the hose, and yep, it's waterproof.

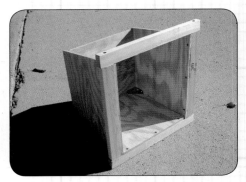

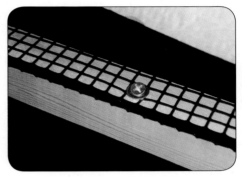

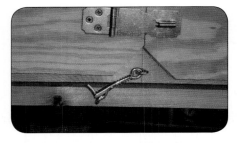

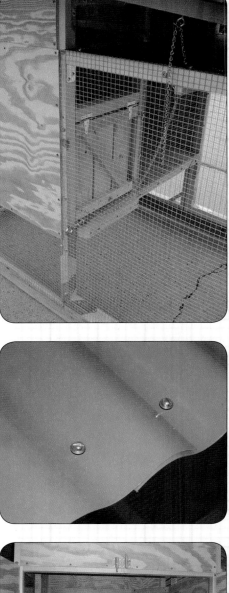

Step 5: Finishing Touches

Well, it's all put together, and now the chickens are chilling out in it. I've added the roost to the henhouse, and put a little "lip" on it to try to keep the bedding in place. The roost is actually another sub-assembly—it's attached to a piece of plywood that screws onto the actual henhouse floor. This is so that I can remove the roost and floor entirely for a couple of different reasons: easier access to get inside the henhouse in case I change my mind about the watering system or need to do any work; for easier cleaning of the floor under the roost (it has 2 to 3 inches of pine bedding underneath it, which I figure will serve about a month before it gets tossed into the composter and new bedding is put down).

I've also added a ramp up to the henhouse door. The chickens spend 99 percent of their time outside, but I think it's because they're pretty dumb creatures and haven't figured out how to jump up inside yet. They have a natural tendency (like all birds) to sleep in the highest possible location, so I'm still scratching my head as to why they'd sleep down in the run when there's a nice cozy roost to sleep in. Maybe this ramp will help out. Sorry, I don't have any photos of it.

The Final Word

I'm sorry if I haven't included specific dimensions for some parts and some of the assemblies here in this Instructable. I figure that if you download the Sketchup file, you can use the measuring tape tool in it to measure stuff out. But anyways, I just wanted to show how easy it is to build something like this, and I'm sure if you're going to build your own you'll come up with your own plan, or use mine as a general template and work your way from there.

A Word About Cost

I started this project with a goal of spending less than $250 for the whole tractor. In actuality, I spent about $270 or so. I *could* have spent a whole lot less by scavenging wood, but that wasn't a consideration at the time. Most of the expense was in the wood. The PVC roofing was rather cheap; I used two pieces at $10 a pop. And were I a better hand at construction, I could have done without all the little angle brackets and stuff.

Author's note:

I used ⅜" plywood for everything but the inner floor. Originally the inner removable floor was ½". I've made a few modifications to the tractor since then—now I've got a single piece of ¾" plywood with linoleum for the removable floor, it adds stability for the roost, and is easier to clean. But the walls and other plywood bits still are the original ⅜".

One other change I might point out—the vinyl roofing is OK, but after having this up for a few months, I don't think the roofing will last. It's already slightly warped in some spots and while it's still keeping out the rain, it looks ugly. If you are ok with the extra weight, or don't plan on moving the tractor often/ever, you might want to consider using a metal roof. It's cheaper, more durable, and will keep the sun/heat out better in the summer; on the other hand, it's heavier.

Collect Rain Water with a Wine Barrel

By Mallie (chout)
(www.instructables.com/id/
Collect-rain-water-with-a-wine-
barrel/)

I think I read all of the Instructables about collecting rain water. Finally decided to build my own with a wine barrel because I didn't want to destroy the look of my future-to-be terrace. I always found rain water collectors super ugly. It's usually an old plastic tank or barrel; handy but not very pleasing to the eye (and I didn't have the motivation to build something like this to hide it). Anyway, here's how I did it.

Material
- a wine barrel (found on eBay for 50 EUR). Make sure to get one with a lid and a cork (usually it's a special cork located in the belly part of the barrel).
- a rain water collector to hook up to the gutter (found on eBay for 19 EUR, but otherwise available in nearly all DIY shops). I chose this model because the collected water would come out via a little tube and not an "open-air" half-pipe
- driller
- flat wood drill heads
- some screws
- an old piece of board about the length of the barrel's lid
- a handle

Step 1: Prepare the Barrel's Lid

Usually the lids of wine barrels are a bit wobbly. They are made of planks inserted into each other and are supposed to be inserted in a groove at the top, inside the barrel. Because of that, I had to make the lid stronger so it would not wear out from frequent usage. I found an old piece of wood board in my garage and screwed it tight at the back of the lid. I made sure to use rustproof (INOX) screws. In order to be able to close the barrel and properly

245

put the lid back on (and because the lid is round), I had to saw the four corners of the board as you can see in the picture. Last year we bought a new kitchen and we received two extra handles (don't ask me why), so I've decided to use one of them for my barrel. The screws that came with the handle weren't long enough to go through the thickness of the lid, plus board attached at the back. So I used a flat drill head to make a wider hole and reduce the thickness so I could properly attach the handle. Make sure to place the handle in the middle of the lid; it's not only more beautiful but also easier to manipulate when you open/close the barrel.

and insert the collector. *Important!* In order to prevent an overflow and avoid my barrel to be overfilled, I installed the rwc a bit lower than the top of the barrel. Therefore the water in the barrel can't go higher than the height on the gutter where the water is collected. I drilled a large hole with the wood flat drill head, inserted the transparent tube that came with the rwc, then used silicon (same as for a shower tub or bath) to seal it and make it waterproof. That way the water could flow back via the tube should it reach a certain level in the barrel.

Step 3: Here Comes the Rain

Within one week my barrel was full to the top (I was even surprised by how much water I had in just a week). I now use it to water my plants and flowers, to wash my terrace, etc. There's still a little bit of wine smell when you open the barrel, but that's more a positive point than a negative one.

Step 2: Connect the Rain Water Collector on the Gutter

I followed the instructions that came with the PVC rain water collector (rwc) to hook it up to one of my gutters. It was super easy; I just had to saw an 8cm section off the gutter at the right height

Green Solar-Powered Water Barrel

By Daniel Moeller (damoelid)
(www.instructables.com/id/
Green-Solar-Powered-Water-
Barrel/)

A green way of using rainwater with the convenience of city water. The attached solar regenerated pump enables you to water plants with pressure, even when the water in the barrels falls low enough that it barely passes the level of the faucet. The sun-warmed water also aids in the growing of plants as it does not shock them. The twin 85-gallon barrels are raised onto a very sturdy 4 × 4 box assembly from recycled wood, held together with new carriage bolts because the total weight of all the water when full is approximately 1700lbs. This frame is resting on eight 2"-thick, 18" square cement pads to prevent sinking. The barrels are raised to increase the head pressure and decrease the work load on the pump.

Step 1: Water Supplied from Mother Nature

Link barrel to downspout. Be sure that the top of barrel remains below level of water entry. I found the Watersaver attachment for the 3 × 4 downspout pipe works perfectly. In order to enable adequate water flow to the barrel, I adapted the Watersaver attachment by drilling out the side and adding a flange for a 1" PVC fitting. I sealed this by using a rubber gasket and additionally using a silicone sealer. Ensure there is a downward slope between the downspout and the barrel entry.

Step 2: Overflow Back to the Downspout

Ensure you have a complete path for water from the downspout to the barrel or barrels and then from the overflow to the downspout again. Use 1" PVC overflow line from the last barrel back to the downspout. Ensure you maintain a drain angle towards the downspout or sediment could collect in the line.

Step 3: Downspout Drain Connection

One-inch PVC entry back into the downspout. Ensure PVC pipe does not fully block the 2" by 3" downspout and keep the downward slope to the pipe to make the water flow towards the downspout.

Step 5: Water Filter

Filter the water from the barrel to protect the pump. This keeps the roof sediment from wearing out the pump. This water filter will last forever, as it has a reusable nylon mesh filter inside that only requires periodic rinsing.

Step 6: Battery Box with Power Switch

Keep the battery and pump protected from the elements inside a full size battery case.

Step 4: Manifold

Common connection point for using water. This photo of the manifold is before I put the water gauge on (shown on intro and last step).

Step 7: Inside View of Battery Box with Motor

An inside view of the standard size battery case and equipment layout. The solar cell was left with clamp connections in order to enable quick removal of the battery case lid for cleaning and maintenance. The pump was recycled from an older sailboat. The battery is a standard size lawn tractor 12V, and with proper maintenance should last six to ten years before needing to be recycled at the depot. An older car battery that just doesn't have the power to crank the car fast enough anymore would be more than adequate for this application and a great alternative to buying a new battery. The 5.5W solar cell was also recycled for a fraction of its original cost from an online classified, and solar cells have a lifespan of approximately fifteen to twenty years. I wanted this little project to last as long as possible before needing any repairs.

Step 8: Flowjet Pump

Close up of Flojet 4405-143. Another pump that I have seen that is almost identical to this is made by Shurflo. This type of pump is used in RVs or sailboats to supply water pressure, as well as for using as a wash down pump on boats. I chose this type because it has an internal pressure switch that stops it from running all the time, only

turning on when the water pressure in the hose drops. In addition I got a super deal on it secondhand. There are many different styles of pumps available that will be more than adequate for this application. It depends on your budget and the availability of secondhand pumps in your area. Other things to consider would be whether or not you want the pump running all the time (lawn sprinkler) or only when you press the trigger on your hose nozzle. Without a built-in pressure switch, the pump will run whenever the power is switched on. In all types of applications, make sure the pump output pressure does not exceed the pressure rating of your hose/pipe or it might burst if the outlet closes or becomes blocked unexpectedly.

Step 9: Water Gauge

As the water level changes inside the barrel, the level inside the tube will follow the same level. This was fun to install as I didn't want to waste all the nice rainwater and drain the tank before I drilled a 3/4" hole in the bottom of the tank to install the angled shut-off valve. I reminded myself to only use a battery powered drill. I reused some half-inch plastic tubing that I had left over from another application and connected it to a 3/4" angle valve with a shut off (which came in handy during install). I sealed around and under all penetrations into the barrel (valve and screws) with a two part epoxy

249

that was a waterproof filler and sealer. It is important to not completely seal the tube or the level will not change to reflect the level in the barrel.

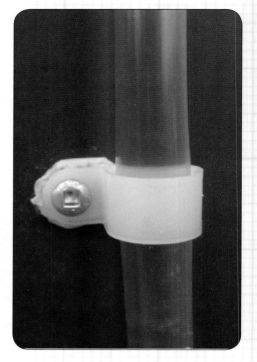

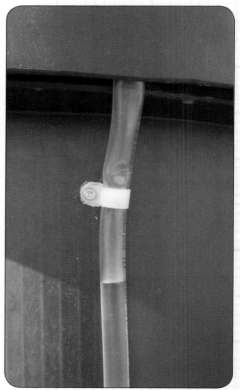

DIY 1000 Watt Wind Turbine

By Steve Spence (sspence)
(www.instructables.com/id/DIY-1000-watt-wind-turbine/)

We built a 1000 watt wind turbine to help charge the battery bank that powers our off-grid home. It's a permanent magnet alternator, generating three-phase AC, rectified to DC, and fed to a charge controller. The magnets spin with the wind and the coils are fixed, so no brushes or slip rings are necessary.

Step 1: Build the Magnet Disks

We had 12" steel disks hydro cut. We cut a template for mounting the magnets. Then we mounted 12-grade n50 magnets around the outside edge. We then built a form, and poured the resin with hardener.

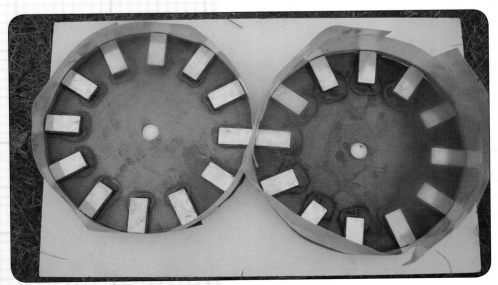

Step 2: Build the Coil Disk

We wound the nine individual coils, soldered them in a three-phase wye configuration, and encased them in resin. We used 35 turns of two parallel strands of 14-gauge enameled (magnet) wire for 12 volts. Use 70 turns of single strand for 24 volts. The three-phase diagram shown here shows three stator coils. Each coil is actually three coils in a series. Coils 1, 4, and 7 are series together, 2, 5, and 8 are series together, and 3, 6, and 9 are series together.

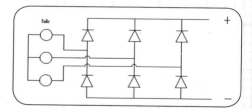

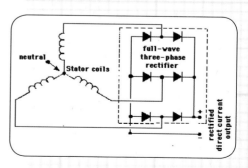

Step 3: Build the Bearing Assembly

Two Harley Davidson wheel bearings are inserted into the pipe, with a smaller pipe locked between them to keep them in place.

Step 4: Construct the Blades

The blades are 2" by 6" pine, cut at 10 degrees on a table saw, and sanded into a rough airfoil. Not perfect, but close enough.

Step 5: Bolt It All Together

How I Built an Electricity-Producing Wind Turbine

By Michael David (mdavis19)
(www.instructables.com/id/How-I-built-an-electricity-producing-wind-turbine/)

Several years ago I bought some remote property in Arizona. I am an astronomer and wanted a place to practice my hobby far away from the terrible light pollution found near cities of any real size. I found a great piece of property. The problem is, it's so remote that there is no electrical service available. That's not really a problem. No electricity equals no light pollution. However, it would be nice to have at least a little electricity, since so much of life in the twenty-first century is dependent on it.

One thing I noticed right away about my property is that most of the time, the wind is blowing. Almost from the moment I bought it, I had the idea of putting up a wind turbine and making some electricity, and later adding some solar panels. This is the story of how I did it. Not with an expensive, store-bought turbine, but with a home-built one that cost hardly anything. If you have some fabricating skills and some electronic know-how, you can build one too.

Step 1: Acquiring a Generator

I started by Googling for information on home-built wind turbines. There are a lot of them out there in an amazing variety of designs and complexities. All of them had five things in common though:

1. A generator
2. Blades
3. A mounting that keeps it turned into the wind
4. A tower to get it up into the wind
5. Batteries and an electronic control system

I reduced the project to just five little systems. If attacked one at a time, the project didn't seem too terribly difficult. I decided to start with the generator. My online research showed that a lot of people were building their own generators. That seemed a bit too complicated, at least for a first effort. Others were using surplus permanent magnet DC motors as generators in their projects. This looked like a simpler way to go. So I began looking into what motors were best for the job. A lot of people seemed to like to use old computer tape drive motors (surplus relics from the days when computers had big reel to reel tape drives). The best apparently are a couple of models of motor made by Ametek. The best motor made by Ametek is a 99 volt DC motor that works great as a generator. Unfortunately, they are almost impossible to locate these days. There are a lot of other Ametek motors around though. A couple of their other models make decent generators and can still be found on places like eBay. I managed to score one of the good 30 volt Ametek motors off of eBay for only $26. They don't go that cheap these days. People are catching on to the fact that they make great wind generators. Other brands will work, so don't fret about the price Ameteks are going for. Shop wisely. Anyway, the motor I got was in good shape and worked great. Even just giving the shaft a quick turn with my fingers would light a 12 volt bulb quite brightly. I gave it a real test by chucking it up in my drill press and connecting it to a dummy load. It works great as a generator, putting out easily a couple hundred watts with this setup. I knew then that if I could make a decent set of blades to drive it, it would produce plenty of power.

me. I followed that general recipe. I did things a little differently though. I used black ABS pipe since my local home center store just happened to have pre-cut lengths of it. I used 6" pipe instead of 4" pipe and 24 inches instead of 19 5/8. I started by quartering a 24-inch piece of pipe around its circumference and cutting it lengthwise into four pieces. Then I cut out one blade, and used it as a template for cutting out the others. That left me with four blades (three plus one spare). I then did a little extra smoothing and shaping using my belt sander and palm sander on the cut edges to try to make them into better airfoils. I don't know if it's really much of an improvement, but it didn't seem to hurt, and the blades look really good (if I do say so myself).

Step 2: Making the Blades

Blades and a hub to connect them to were the next order of business. More online research ensued. A lot of people made their own blades by carving them out of wood. That looked like an outrageous amount of work to me. I found that other people were making blades by cutting sections out of PVC pipe and shaping them into airfoils. That looked a lot more promising to

Step 3: Building the Hub

Next I needed a hub to bolt the blades to and attach to the motor. Rummaging around in my workshop, I found a toothed pulley that fit on the motor shaft, but was a little too small in diameter to bolt the blades onto. I also found a scrap disk of aluminum 5 inches in diameter and 1/4" thick that I could bolt the blades onto, but wouldn't attach to the motor shaft. The simple solution of course was to bolt these two pieces together to make the hub. Much drilling, tapping, and bolting later, I had a hub.

Step 4: Building the Turbine Mounting

Next I needed a mounting for the turbine. Keeping it simple, I opted to just strap the motor to a piece of 2 × 4 wood. The correct length of the wood was computed by the highly scientific method of picking the best looking piece of scrap 2 × 4 off my scrap wood pile and going with however long it was. I also cut a piece of 4" diameter PVC pipe to make a shield to go over the motor and protect it from the weather. For a tail to keep it turned into the wind, I again just used a piece of heavy sheet aluminum I happened to have laying around. I was worried that it wouldn't be a big enough tail, but it seems to work just fine. The turbine snaps right around into the wind every time it changes direction. I have added a few dimensions to the picture. I doubt any of these measurements are critical though. Next, I had to begin thinking about some sort of tower and some sort of bearing that would allow the head to freely turn into the wind. I spent a lot of time in my local home center stores (Lowes and Home Depot) brainstorming. Finally, I came up with a solution that seems to work well. While brainstorming, I noticed that 1" diameter iron pipe is a good slip-fit inside 1 1/4" diameter steel EMT electrical conduit. I could use a long piece of 1 1/4" conduit as my tower and 1" pipe fittings at either end. For the head unit I attached a 1" iron floor flange centered 7 ½ inches back from the generator end of the 2 × 4, and screwed a 10"-long iron pipe nipple into it. The nipple would slip into the top of the piece of conduit I'd use as a tower and form a nice bearing. Wires from the generator would pass through a hole drilled in the 2 × 4 down the center of the pipe/conduit unit and exit at the base of the tower.

Step 5: Build the Tower Base

For the tower base, I started by cutting a 2' diameter disk out of plywood. I made a U-shaped assembly out of 1" pipe fittings. In the middle of that assembly I put a 1 1/4" tee. The tee is free to turn around the 1" pipe and forms a hinge that allows me to raise and lower the tower. I then added a close nipple, a 1¼ to 1 reducing fitting, and a 12" nipple. Later I added a 1" tee between the reducer and the 12" nipple so there would be a place for the wires to exit the pipe. This is shown in a photo further down the page. I also later drilled holes in the wooden disk to allow me to use steel stakes to lock it in place on the ground. The second photo shows the head and base together. You can begin to see how it will go together. Imagine a 10' piece of steel conduit connecting the two pieces. Since I was building this thing in Florida, but was going to use it in Arizona, I decided to hold off on purchasing the 10' piece of conduit until I got to Arizona. That meant the wind turbine would not be fully assembled and would not get properly tested until I was ready to put it up in the field. That was a little scary because I wouldn't know if the thing actually worked until I tried it in Arizona.

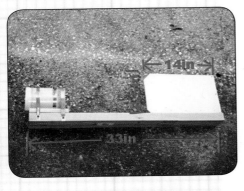

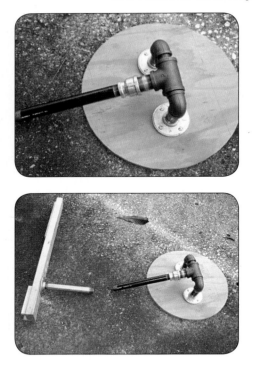

Step 7: The Finished Head of the Wind Turbine

This photo shows the finished head unit with the blades attached. Is that a thing of beauty or what? It almost looks like I know what I'm doing. I never got a chance to properly test the unit before heading to Arizona. One windy day though, I did take the head outside and hold it high up in the air above my head into the wind just to see if the blades would spin as well as I had hoped. Spin they did. In a matter of a few seconds, the blades spun up to a truly scary speed (no load on the generator), and I found myself holding onto a giant, spinning, whirligig of death, with no idea how to put it down without getting myself chopped to bits. Fortunately, I did eventually manage to turn it out of the wind and slow it down to a non-lethal speed. I won't make that mistake again.

Step 6: Paint All the Wooden Parts

Next, I painted all the wooden parts with a couple of coats of white latex paint I had leftover from another project. I wanted to protect the wood from the weather. This photo also shows the lead counterweight I added to the left side of the 2 × 4 under the tail to balance the head.

Step 8: Build the Charge Controller

Now that I had all the mechanical parts sorted out, it was time to turn toward the electronic end of the project. A wind power system consists of the wind turbine, one or more batteries to store power produced by the turbine, a blocking diode to prevent power from the batteries being wasted spinning the motor/generator, a secondary load to dump power from the turbine into when

the batteries are fully charged, and a charge controller to run everything. There are lots of controllers for solar and wind power systems. Anyplace that sells alternative energy stuff will have them. There are also always a lot of them for sale on eBay. I decided to try building my own though. So it was back to Googling for information on wind turbine charge controllers. I found a lot of information, including some complete schematics, which was quite nice and made building my own unit very easy. Again, while I followed a general recipe from an online source, I did do some things differently. Being an avid electronics tinkerer from an early age, I have a huge stock of electronic components already on hand, so I had to buy very little to complete the controller. I substituted different components for some parts and reworked the circuit a little just so I could use parts I already had on hand. That way I had to buy almost nothing to build the controller. The only part I had to buy was the relay. I built my prototype charge controller by bolting all the pieces to a piece of plywood, as seen in the first photo below. I would rebuild it in a weatherproof enclosure later. Whether you build your own or buy one, you will need some sort of controller for your wind turbine. The general principal behind the controller is that it monitors the voltage of the battery(s) in your system, and either sends power from the turbine into the batteries to recharge them or dumps the power from the turbine into a secondary load if the batteries are fully charged (to prevent over-charging and destroying the batteries). In operation, the wind turbine is connected to the controller. Lines then run from the controller to the battery. All loads are taken directly from the battery. If the battery voltage drops below 11.9 volts, the controller switches the turbine power to charging the

battery. If the battery voltage rises to 14 volts, the controller switches to dumping the turbine power into the dummy load. There are trimpots to adjust the voltage levels at which the controller toggles back and forth between the two states. I chose 11.9V for the discharge point and 14V for the fully charged point based on advice from different web sites on the subject of properly charging lead acid batteries. The sites all recommended slightly different voltages. I sort of averaged them and came up with my numbers. When the battery voltage is between 11.9V and 14.8V, the system can be switched between either charging or dumping. A pair of push buttons allow me to switch between states anytime, for testing purposes. Normally the system runs automatically. When charging the battery, the yellow LED is lit. When the battery is charged and power is being dumped to the dummy load, the green LED is lit. This gives me some minimal feedback on what is going on with the system. I also use my multimeter to measure both battery voltage and turbine output voltage. I will probably eventually add either panel meters or automotive-style voltage and charge/discharge meters to the system. I'll do that once I have it in some sort of enclosure. I used my variable voltage bench power supply to simulate a battery in various states of charge and discharge to test and tune the controller. I could set the voltage of the power supply to 11.9V and set the trimpot for the low voltage trip point. Then I could crank the voltage up to 14V and set the trimpot for the high voltage trimpot. I had to get it set before I took it into the field because I'd have no way to tune it up out there. I have found out the hard way that it is important with this controller design to connect the battery first, and then connect the wind turbine and/or solar panels. If you connect the wind turbine first, the wild voltage swings coming from the turbine won't be smoothed out by the load of the battery, the controller will behave erratically, the relay will click away wildly, and voltage spikes could destroy the ICs. So always connect to the battery(s) first, and then connect the wind turbine. Also, make sure you disconnect the wind turbine first when taking the system apart. Disconnect the battery(s) last.

Step 9: Erect the Tower

At last, all parts of the project were complete. It was all done only a week before my vacation arrived. That was cutting it close. I disassembled the turbine and carefully packed the parts and the tools I'd need to assemble it for their trip across the country. Then I once again I drove out to my remote property in Arizona for a week of off-grid relaxation, but this time with hopes of having some actual electricity on the site. The first order of business was setting up and bracing the tower. After arriving at my property and unloading my van, I drove to the nearest Home Depot (about 60 miles one way) and bought the 10' piece of 1 1/4" conduit I needed for the tower. Once I had it, assembly went quickly. I used nylon rope to anchor the pole to four big wooden stakes driven in the ground. Turnbuckles on the lower

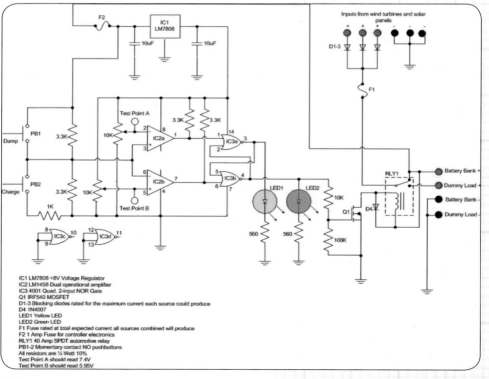

ends of each guy-line allowed me to plumb up the tower. By releasing the line from either stake in line with the hinge at the base, I could raise and lower the tower easily. Eventually the nylon line and wooden stakes will be replaced with steel stakes and steel cables. For testing though, this arrangement worked fine. The second photo shows a close-up of how the guy-lines attach near the top of the tower. I used chain-link fence brackets as tie points for my guy-lines. The fence brackets don't quite clamp down tightly on the conduit, which is smaller in diameter than the fence posts they are normally used with. So there is a steel hose clamp at either end of the stack of brackets to keep them in place. The third photo shows the base of the tower, staked to the ground, with the wire from the wind turbine exiting from the tee below the conduit tower. I used an old orange extension cord with a broken plug to connect between the turbine and the controller. I simply cut both ends off and put on spade lugs. Threading the wire through the tower turned out to be easy. It was a cold morning and the cord was very stiff. I was able to just push it through the length of the conduit tower. On a warmer day I probably would have had to use a fish tape or string line to pull the cord through the conduit. I got lucky.

Step 10: Erect the Wind Turbine

The first photo shows the turbine head installed on top of the tower. I greased up the pipe on the bottom of the head and slid it into the top of the conduit. It made a great bearing, just as I'd planned. Sometimes I even amaze myself. Too bad there was nobody around to get an Iwo Jima Flag Raising-type picture of me raising the tower up with the head installed. The second photo shows the wind turbine fully assembled. Now I'm just waiting for the wind to blow. Wouldn't you know it, it was dead calm that morning. It was the first calm day I had ever seen out there. The wind had always been blowing every other time I had been there.

Step 11: Connect the Electronics

The first photo below shows the electronics setup. The battery, inverter, meter, and prototype charge controller are all sitting on a plywood board on top of a blue plastic tub. I plug a long extension cord into the inverter and run power back to my campsite. Once the wind starts blowing, the turbine head snaps around into it and begins spinning up. It spins up quickly until the output voltage exceeds the battery voltage plus the blocking diode drop (around 13.2 volts, depending on the state of the battery charge). It is really running without a load until that point. Once that voltage is exceeded, the turbine suddenly has a load as it begins dumping power into the battery. Once under load, the RPMs only slightly increase as the wind speed increases. More wind means more current into the battery which means more load on the generator. So the system is pretty much self-governing. I saw no signs of over-revving. Of course, in storm-force winds, all bets are off. Switching the controller to dump power into the dummy load did a good job of braking the turbine and slowing it way down even in stronger gusts. Actually shorting the turbine output is an even better brake. It brings the turbine to a halt even in strong winds. Shorting the output is how I made the turbine safe to raise and lower, so I wouldn't get sliced and diced by the spinning blades. Warning though, the whole head assembly can still swing around and crack you hard on the noggin if the wind changes direction while you are working on these things. So be careful out there.

Step 12: Enjoy Having Power in the Middle of Nowhere

How sweet it is! I have electricity! Here I have my laptop computer set up and plugged into the power provided by the inverter, which in turn is powered by the wind turbine. I normally only have about two hours of battery life on my laptop. So I don't get to use it much while I'm camping. It comes in handy though for downloading photos out of my camera when its memory card gets full, making notes on projects like this one, working on the next great American novel, or just watching DVD movies. Now I have no battery life problems, at least as long as the wind blows. Besides the laptop, I can also now recharge all my other battery powered equipment like my cell phone, my camera, my electric shaver, my air mattress pump, etc. Life used to get real primitive on previous camping trips when the batteries in all my electronic stuff ran down. I used the wind turbine to power my new popup trailer on a later vacation. The strong spring winds kept the wind turbine spinning all day every day and most of the nights too while I was in Arizona. The turbine provided enough power for the interior 12V lighting and enough for 120V AC at the power outlets to keep my battery charger, electric shaver, and mini vacuum cleaner (camping is messy) all charged up and running. My girlfriend complained about it not having enough power to run her hairdryer though.

Step 13: How Much Did It Cost?

So how much did all this cost to build? Well, I saved all the receipts for everything I bought related to this project.

Part	Origin	Cost
Motor/ generator	eBay	$26.00
Misc. pipe fittings	Homecenter Store	$41.49
Pipe for blades	Homecenter Store	$12.84
Misc hardware	Homecenter Store	$8.00
Conduit	Homecenter Store	$19.95
Wood and aluminum	Scrap Pile	$0.00
Power cable	Old extension cord	$0.00
Rope and turnbuckles	Homecenter Store	$18.47
Electronic parts	Already on hand	$0.00
Relay	Auto Parts Store	$13.87
Battery	Borrowed from my UPS	$0.00
Inverter	Already on hand	$0.00
Paint	Already on hand	$0.00
Total		$140.62

Not too bad. I doubt I could buy a commercially made turbine with a comparable power output, plus a commercially made charge controller, plus a commercially made tower for less than $750-$1000.

added a built in voltage meter. Both were bought cheap on eBay. I have also added a few new features. The unit now has provisions for power inputs from multiple sources. It also has built-in fused 12V power distribution for three external loads.

The second photo shows the inside of the charge controller. I basically just transferred everything that I originally had bolted onto the plywood board in the prototype into this box. I added an automotive illuminated voltage gauge and fuses for three external 12V loads. I used heavy gauge wire to try to reduce losses due to wire resistance. Every watt counts when you are living off-grid.

The third image is the schematic for the new charge controller. It is pretty much the same as the old one above, except for the addition of the volt meter and extra fuse blocks for the external loads.

The photo directly below is a block diagram of the whole power system.

Step 14: Extras

I have completed the rebuild of the charge controller. It is now in a semi-weatherproof enclosure, and I have also

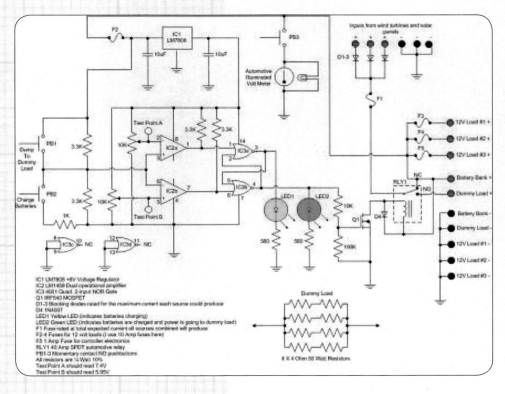

Note that I only have one solar panel built right now. I just haven't had the time to complete the second one.

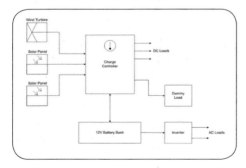

Step 15: More Extras

Once again I stayed on my remote property during my recent vacation in Arizona. This time I had both my home-built wind turbine and my home-built solar panel with me. Working together, they provided plenty of power for my (admittedly minimal) electricity needs.

The second photo shows the new charge controller unit. The wires on the left side are coming from the wind turbine and solar panel. The wires on the right side are going to the battery bank and dummy load. I cut up an old heavy-duty 100' extension cord to make cables to connect wind turbine and solar panel to the charge controller. The cable to the wind turbine is about 75 feet long and the cable to the solar panel is about 25 feet long. The battery bank I am currently using consists of eleven sealed lead-acid 12V batteries of 8 Amp-Hour capacity connected in parallel. That gives me 88 Amp-Hours of storage capacity, which is plenty for camping. As long as it is sunny and windy, (nearly every day is sunny and windy on my property), the wind turbine and solar panel keep the batteries well charged.

Build a 60 Watt Solar Panel

By Michael Davis (mdavid19)
(www.instructables.com/id/
Build-a-60-Watt-
Solar-Panel/)

Several years ago I bought some remote property in Arizona. I am an astronomer and wanted a place to practice my hobby far away from the terrible light pollution found near cities of any real size. I found a great piece of property. The problem is, it's so remote that there is no electricity available. That's not really a problem. No electricity equals no light pollution. However, it would be nice to have at least a little electricity, since so much of life in the twenty-first century is dependent on it.

I built a wind turbine to provide some power on the remote property (will be another Instructable in the future). It works great, when the wind blows. However, I wanted more power and more dependable power. The wind seems to blow all the time on my property, except when I really need it to. I do get well over three hundred sunny days a year on the property though, so solar power seemed like the obvious choice to supplement the wind turbine. Solar panels are very expensive though. So I decided to try my hand at building my own. I used common tools and inexpensive and easy to acquire materials to build a solar panel that rivals commercial panels in power production, but completely blows them away in price. Read on for step-by-step instructions on how I did it.

Step 1: Buy Some Solar Cells

I bought a couple of bricks of 3 × 6 mono-crystalline solar cells. It takes a total of 36 of these type solar cells wired in series to make a panel. Each cell produces about ½ volt. Thirty-six in a series would give about 18 volts, which would be good for charging 12 volt batteries. (Yes, you really need that high a voltage to effectively charge 12 volt batteries.) This type of solar cell is as thin as paper and as brittle and fragile as glass. They are very easily damaged. The eBay seller of the cells I purchased dipped stacks of 18 in wax to stabilize them and make it easier to ship them without damaging them. The wax is quite a pain to remove though. If you can, find cells for sale that aren't dipped in wax. Keep in mind though that they may suffer some more damage in shipping. Notice that these cells have metal tabs on them. You want cells with tabs on them. You are already going to have to do a lot of soldering to build a panel from tabbed solar cells. If you buy cells without tabs, it will at least double the amount of soldering you have to do. So pay extra for tabbed cells.

I also bought a couple of lots of cells that weren't dipped in wax from another eBay seller. These cells came packed in a plastic box. They rattled around in the box and got a little chipped up on the edges and corners. Minor chips don't really matter too much. They won't reduce the cell's output enough to worry about. These are all blemished and factory seconds anyway. The main reason solar cells get rejected is for chips. So what's another chip or two? All together I bought enough cells to make two panels. I knew I'd probably break or otherwise ruin at least a few during construction, so I bought extras.

Step 2: Build the Box

So what is a solar panel anyway? It is basically a box that holds an array of solar cells. So I started out by building myself a shallow box. I made the box shallow so the sides won't shade the solar cells when the sun comes at an angle. It is made of 3/8"-thick plywood with 3/4 × 3/4 pieces of wood around the edges. The pieces are glued and screwed in place. This panel will hold 36 3 × 6 inch solar cells. I decided to make two sub-panels of 18 cells each just so make it easier to assemble. I knew I would be working at my kitchen table when I would be soldering the cells together, and would have limited work space. So there is a center divider

across the middle of the box. Each sub-panel will fit into one well in the main panel. The second photo is my sort of back of the envelope sketch showing the overall dimensions of the solar panel. All dimensions are in inches (sorry you fans of the metric system). The side pieces are 3/4 by 3/4 and go all the way around the edges of the plywood substrate. Also a piece goes across the center to divide the panel into two sub-panels. This is just the way I chose to do it. There is nothing critical about these dimensions, or even the overall design.

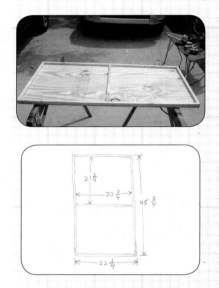

Step 3: Finishing the Box

Here is a close-up showing one half of the main panel. This well will hold one 18-cell sub-panel. Notice the little holes drilled in the edges of the well. This will be the bottom of the panel (it is upside down in the photo). These are vent holes to keep the air pressure inside the panel equalized with the outside, and to let moisture escape. These holes must be on the bottom of the panel or rain and dew will run inside. There must also be vent holes in the center divider between the two sub panels. After using the panel for a while, I now recommend that the vent holes be increased to at least ¼" in diameter. Also, to keep dust and critters out of the panel, stuff a little fiberglass insulation in the holes in the bottom rail of the panel. The insulation is not needed in the holes in the center divider.

Next I cut two pieces of Masonite peg board to fit inside the wells. These pieces of pegboard will be the substrates that each sub-panel will be built on. They were cut to be a loose fit in the wells. You don't have to use peg board for this. I just happened to have some on hand. Just about any thin, rigid and non-conducting material should work. To protect the solar cells from the weather, the panel will have a Plexiglas front. In the third picture, two pieces of scrap Plexiglas have been cut to fit the front of the panel. I didn't have one piece big enough to do the whole thing. Glass could also be used for this, but glass is fragile. Hail stones and flying debris that would shatter glass will just bounce off the Plexi. Now you can start to see what the finished panel will look like.

Step 4: Paint the Box

Next I gave all the wooden parts of the panel several coats of paint to protect them from moisture and the weather. The box was painted inside and out. The type of paint and color was scientifically chosen by shaking all the paint cans I had laying around in my garage and choosing the one that felt like it had enough left in it to do the whole job. The peg board pieces were also painted. They got several coats on both sides. Be sure to paint them on both sides or they will warp when exposed to moisture. Warping could damage the solar cells that will be glued to them.

Step 5: Prepare the Solar Cells

Now that I had the structure of the panel finished, it was time to get the solar cells ready. As I said above, getting the wax off the cells is a real pain. After some trial and error, I came up with a way that works fairly well. Still, I would recommend buying from someone who doesn't dip their cells in wax. This photo shows the complete setup I used. My girlfriend asked what I was cooking. Imagine her surprise when I said solar cells. The initial hot water bath for melting the wax is in the right-rear. On the left-front is a bath of hot soapy water. On the right-front is a bath of hot clean water. All the pots are at just below boiling temperature. The sequence I used was to melt the bricks apart in the hot water bath on the right-rear. I'd tease the cells apart and transfer them one at a time to the soapy water bath on the left-front to remove any wax on the cell. Then the cell would be given a rinse in the hot clean water on the right-front. The cells would then be set out to dry on a towel. You should change the water frequently in the soapy and rinse water baths. Don't pour the water down the sink though, because the wax will solidify in your drains and clog them up. Dump the water outside. This process removed almost all the wax from the cells. There is still a very light film on some of the cells, but it doesn't seem to interfere with soldering or the working of the cells. Don't let the water boil in any of the pans or the bubbles will jostle the cells against each other violently. Also, boiling water may be hot enough to loosen the electrical connections on the cells. I also recommend putting the brick of cells in the water cold, and then slowly heating it up to just below boiling temperature to avoid harsh thermal shocks to the cells. Plastic tongs and spatulas come in handy for teasing the

cells apart once the wax melts. Try not to pull too hard on the metal tabs or they may rip off. I found that out the hard way while trying to separate the cells. Good thing I bought extras.

Step 6: Solder the Solar Cells Together

I started out by drawing a grid pattern on each of the two pieces of pegboard, lightly in pencil, so I would know where each of the 18 cells would be located. Then I laid out the cells on that grid pattern upside-down so I could solder them together. All 18 cells on each half panel need to be soldered together in series, and then both half panels need to be connected in series to get the desired voltage. Soldering the cells together was tricky at first, but I got the hang of it fairly quickly. Start out with just two cells upside-down. Lay the solder tabs from the front of one cell across the solder points on the back of the other cell. I made sure the spacing between the cells matched the grid pattern. I continued this until I had a line of six cells soldered together. I then soldered tabs from scrapped solar cells to the solder points on the last cell in the string. Then I made two more lines of six cells. I used a low-wattage soldering iron and fine rosin-core solder. I also used a rosin pen on the solder points on the back of the cells before soldering. Use a really light touch with the soldering iron. The cells are thin and delicate. If you push too hard, you will break the cells. I got careless a couple of times and had to scrap a couple of cells.

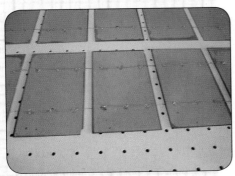

Step 7: Glue Down the Solar Cells

Gluing the cells in place proved to be a little tricky. I placed a small blob of clear silicone caulk in the center of each cell in a six-cell string. Then I flipped the string over and set in place on the pencil line grid I had laid out earlier. I pressed lightly in the center of each cell to get it to stick to the pegboard panel. Flipping the floppy string of cells is tricky. Another set of hands may be useful in during this step. Don't use too much glue, and don't glue the cells anywhere but at their centers. The cells and the panel they are mounted on will expand, contract, flex, and warp with changes in temperature and humidity. If glue the cells too tightly to the substrate, they will crack in time. Gluing them at only one point in the center allows the cells to float freely on top of the substrate. Both can expand and flex more or less independently, and the delicate solar cells won't crack. Next time I will do it differently. I will solder tabs onto the backs of all the solar cells. Then I will glue all the cells down in their proper places. Then I will solder the tabs together. It seems like the obvious way to go to me now, but I had to do it the hard way once to figure it out. Here is one half panel, finally finished.

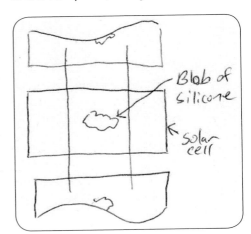

Blob of silicone

Solar cell

Step 8: Interconnect the Strings of Solar Cells and Test the Half Panel

Here I used copper braid to interconnect first and second strings of cells. You could use solar cell tabbing material or even regular wire. I just happened to have the braid on hand. There is another similar interconnection between the second and third strings at the opposite end of the board. I used blobs of silicone caulk to anchor the braid and prevent it from flopping around. The second photo shows a test of the first half panel outside in the sun. In weak sun through clouds the half panel is producing 9.31 volts. It works! Now all I had to do is build another one just like it. Once I had two half panels complete, I installed them in their places in the main panel frame and wired them together.

Step 9: Install the Half Panels in the Box

Each of the half panels dropped right into their places in the main panel frame. I used four small screws (like the silver one in the photo) to anchor each of the half panels in place.

Step 10: Interconnect the Two Half Panels

Wires to connect the two half panels together were run through the vent holes in the central divider. Again, blobs of silicone caulk were used to anchor the wire in place and prevent it from flopping around.

Step 11: Install the Blocking Diode

Each solar panel in a solar power system needs a blocking diode in series with it to prevent the panel from discharging your batteries at night or during cloudy weather. I used a Schottky diode with a 3.3 amp current rating. Schottky diodes have a much lower forward voltage drop than ordinary rectifier diodes, so less power is wasted. Every watt counts when you are off-grid. I got a package of 25 31DQ03 Schottky diodes on eBay for only a few bucks. So I have enough leftovers for lots more solar panels

My original plan was to mount the diode in line with the positive wire outside the panel. After looking at the spec-sheet for the diode though, I decided to mount it inside since the forward voltage drop gets lower as the temperature rises. It will be warmer inside the panel and the diode will work more efficiently. More silicone caulk was used to anchor the diode and wires.

Step 12: Run Wires Outside and Put on the Plexiglas Covers

I drilled a hole in the back of the panel near the top for the wires to exit. I put a knot in the wires for strain relief and anchored them in place with yet more of the silicone caulk.

It is important to let all the silicone caulk cure well before screwing the Plexiglas covers in place. I have found through past experience that the fumes from the caulk may leave a film on the inside of the Plexiglas and on the cells if it isn't allowed to thoroughly cure in the open air before you screw on the covers.

And still more silicone caulk was used to seal the outside of the panel where the wires exit.

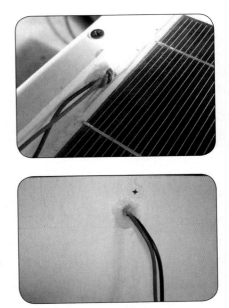

Step 13: Add a Plug

I added a polarized two-pin Jones plug to the end of the panel wires. A mating female plug will be wired into the charge controller I use with my home-built wind turbine so the solar panel can supplement its power production and battery-charging capacity.

Step 14: The Completed Panel

Here is the completed panel with the Plexiglas covers screwed into place. It isn't sealed shut yet at this point. I wanted to wait until after testing it because was worried that I might have to get back inside it if there were problems. Sure enough, a tab popped off one of the cells. Maybe it was due to thermal stresses or shock from handling. Who knows? I opened up the panel and replaced that one cell. I haven't had any more trouble since. I will probably seal the panel with either a bead of silicone caulk, or aluminum AC duct tape wrapped around the edges.

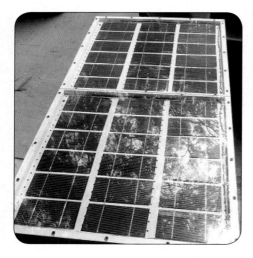

Step 15: Testing the Solar Panel

The first photo shows the voltage output of the completed panel in bright winter sunlight. My meter says 18.88 volts with no load. That's exactly what I was aiming for. In the second photo I am testing the current capacity of the panel, again in bright winter sunlight. My meter says 3.05 amps short circuit current. That is right about what the cells are rated for. So the panel is working very well.

Step 16: Using the Solar Panel

Here is a photo of the solar panel in action, providing much needed power on my remote Arizona property. I used an old extension cord to bring the power from the panel located in a sunny clearing over to my campsite under the trees. I cut the original ends off the cord and installed Jones plugs. You could stick with the original 120V connectors, but I wanted to make sure there was absolutely no chance of accidentally plugging the low-voltage DC equipment into 120V AC. I have to move the panel several times each day to keep it pointed at the sun, but that isn't really a big hardship. Maybe someday I will build a tracking system to automatically keep it aimed at the sun.

sorts of building supplies and hardware. I also have a lot of useful scrap pieces of wood, wire, and all sorts of miscellaneous stuff (some would say junk) laying around the shop. So I had a lot of stuff on hand already. Your mileage may vary.

Part:	Origin:	Cost:
Solar cells	eBay	$74.00*
Misc. lumber	Home Center Store	$20.62
Plexiglas	Scrap Pile	$0.00
Screws and misc. hardware	Already on hand	$0.00
Silicone caulk	Home Center Store	$3.95
Wire	Already on hand	$0.00
Diode	eBay	$0.20+
Jones plug	Newark Electronics	$6.08
Paint	Already on hand	$0.00

Total: $104.85

Not too bad! That's a fraction of what a commercially made solar panel with a comparable power output would cost, and it was easy. I already have plans to build more panels to add to the capacity of my system.

I actually bought four lots of 18 solar cells on eBay. This price represents only the two lots that went into building this panel. Also, the price of factory second solar cells on eBay has gone up quite a lot recently as oil prices have skyrocketed.

This price represents one out of a lot of 25 diodes I bought on eBay for $5.00.

Step 17: Counting the Cost

So how much did all this cost to build? Well, I saved all the receipts for everything I bought related to this project. Also, my workshop is well stocked with all

How to Make PV Solar Panels

By viron
(www.instructables.com/id/How-to-MAKE-PV-Solar-Panels/)

This is not "How to Make PV Solar *Cells*". It is possible to home-make Copper Oxide and other kinds of materials, but that is a whole other story, which I may do in the future. It might be a little ambitious to explain how I made PV solar panels out of various types of cells, how and where I obtained those cells inexpensively, the differences in various kinds of cells, and how to work with them to get free electricity from the sun and other sources of light. In essence, this involves ways to connect cells, which may produce more or less than one volt. Also, you are not only trying to increase

power output but also decrease the load; that is, efficiently conserve the energy whether it is meager or significant. For example, even the weakest solar panels can run watches, calculators, and radios, charge batteries, and, if it were specifically designed to, power a computer as it would a calculator. Here are some pictures of Solar Panels that I have constructed.

Supplies and Sources

What you may be able to use to build a useful solar panel:

- "Broken" solar cells. They are very cheap and they work, they are just randomly shaped. They are usually crystalline silicon ones, which *always* look broken even when they are not.
- Surplus solar cells: Amorphous silicon printed on glass are excellent, usually producing more than a volt, and much sturdier than the thin ones that break in bulk quantities. If these break, they usually can be fixed.

- Indium Copper Selenide Cells: These are "new" and are conveniently sold as glass tiles with easy to solder tabs.
- Any of the above, sold as cells prepared for assembly into panels; in other words, complete and solder-ready or with wires and tabs. (I will explain how to prepare inferior quality cells in this Instructable.)
  Miscellaneous items:
- wire glue—There is already another Instructable for using wire glue on broken solar cells.
- brass extrusions bracket |_| shaped—Convenient for connecting to glass cells.
- solder
- soldering iron—low wattage
- small flat-head screwdriver
- thin (around 20 AWG or less) stranded copper wire
- lamp cord or speaker wire
- alligator clips
- deep picture frames or shadow boxes—look for imported frames at the El Cheapo store and pray a machine made them
- acrylic/Lexan/Plexiglas/etc. clear polymer sheets
- router or Dremel to cut out the middle of one out of three sheets
- RTV (Silicone Glue) or high temperature hot melt glue (Caution—you don't want the sun to melt it!)
- Rectifier diode such as 1N4001 or 1N4004
- voltage doubler or multiplier circuits (you can make) to increase voltage output—examples: ICL7660, MAX1044, MAX232, etc.
- wide sticky tape
- double sticky foam tape
- rechargeable nickel batteries
- gel cells or car battery (you have one, might as well use it until it's useless)—Li-Ion are not recommended because they are harder to charge

- analog volt meter (only because it doesn't need batteries like a digital one)
- AC inverter—if you are charging a powerful battery and would occasionally run some main-powered appliances. Some UPSs can be easily modified to be inverters, if they can be turned on after a power failure.
  Sources:
  Broken Solar Cells:
  Herbach and Rademan
  Silicon Solar
  Electronic Goldmine Glass (Amorphous) Solar Cells:
  Electronic Goldmine
  Note: Other stores listed may also supply glass solar cells.
  Indium Copper Selenide Cells.
  All Electronics
  Edmund Scientific
  Electronic Goldmine

Other sources

Cheap weather damaged solar powered outdoor night lights—(common failures are circuit corrosion and defective batteries, not the solar cells). Defective solar calculators, solar charged flashlights, etc.

Perhaps a little off topic

For a reasonably good deal on Complete and Useful Solar Panels I recommend "Solar Car Battery Chargers" that are about one or two watts and between $20 and $30 whenever an opportunity to get some arises. But those are what I am trying to show how to make an approximate equivalent of.

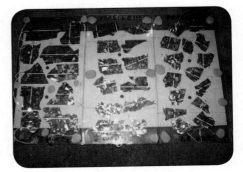

Step 1: How to Use "Broken" Cells

They are the crystalline ones that always look broken, but if they really are, then they have not been fully prepared for use. It is an extra challenge to solder wires onto them but this is how I do it: Look for the wide line on the pieces, and sort out ones that only have thin lines. The thin line ones might be useful with wire glue but are too hard to solder. Then sort the pieces with wide lines by how big they are. They will all be about 0.55 volts, but the larger pieces make more current than the smaller pieces, and it's nice to have a panel with consistent current, especially the one you make with the biggest pieces. Let's save the big pieces until we learn what to do with the small pieces. Strip apart a short length of stranded wire and put the now loose strands in a small box just so you can find them and so they don't wander into another project and cause a short circuit. Actually, another option may be to use wire-wrap wire instead of bare strands, if you don't mind stripping the end of each piece. The broken cells have a very thin conductive layer on the blue side and a very rough, thicker one on the other. It will be more challenging to solder onto them than on perfect cells but this is how. First the blue side. . .

Step 2: Preparing Broken Cells

If you can solder onto the cells then they are higher quality than the ones I have so you can skip these preparing steps. On the blue side, scratch the thick line with a very small flat screwdriver with just a little force so that the cell doesn't break, and the line should turn from white to shiny unless it's already shiny and ready to solder. Try to make a little shiny circle. We will solder there. Make the flat edge of the screwdriver completely touch the scratched area so it rubs wide. Mostly push back and forth so that the rubbing removes the thin oxidation. After scratching the line, turn the cell and scratch the circle back and forth again. Maybe turn it once more and scratch it once more. Now flip the cell over and notice the rough stuff on the back. If there appears to be two different roughnesses or shades of grey, we are going to scratch in two places. Again, turn the cell and scratch it in one or two little circles by pushing the edge of the screwdriver up and down to remove the coating that solder won't stick to. Now back to the blue side. Try to get a solder ball to stick. If it does not stick, and rosin gunks up the area, scrape it off and try again, and if it seems hopeless, scrape another part of the wide line on the cell. I did not have that problem because of practice. Now try to put a bump of solder in the two places scratched on the bottom of the cell. I was only able to get one bump to stick. There are areas on the bottom where solder just won't stick. But if neither spot sticks, try scraping the rosin off the spots and soldering again, or carefully scratching another spot. If you have a bump on the blue side, it's good but you can't lay the cell flat now. The spot that worked was rougher and thicker than the one that didn't, and that means there's a lot more silver there, and more likely it will solder.

Now that you have two solder bumps, you can attach two thin wires, either strands from stranded wire or thin wire-wrap wire. What about thicker wire? It can pull the lines off the cell and then you can forget about soldering it. Put it in the "wire glue" bin. Now that there are two wires on the cell, test it with a meter. The blue side of the cell will make up to 0.55 negative volts, so connect the meter PLUS to the wire on the silver-gray bottom of the cell. My cell isn't getting much light but the meter needle is indicating that it is making electricity.

Step 3: "Broken" or "Crystalline" Cell Panels

In the last step I mentioned that the blue side is negative and the silver side is positive. Now all you have to do is solder your cells in series to get more voltage. To do that you only need one more wire for each additional cell you add. Remember each cell makes up to half a volt, so consider a 12 volt panel to have 24 or more cells. A few extra is good. One reason for that is a diode lowers the voltage just a little bit, and another is that it's nice to have 12 volts for charging batteries when it's not the sunniest time of day. A diode is used when the panel charges batteries, so the batteries don't give any power back to the panel in the dark. That would be a waste of free power. Because the cells are so fragile, it would be good to install them in a deep picture frame (shadow box) with double stick foam tape or RTV glue. Be careful, this is permanent. You could make it less permanent with hot-melt glue also. At this point you don't need to think that the cells are "already broken," and you will have a well working panel. You could hide the shard-shapes with fluorescent lighting diffraction plastic over the framed panel if you like. Perhaps you've seen a shard-cell panel just like that being sold before.

Step 4: Preparing Glass (Amorphous) Cells

I received a surplus glass cells with instructions on how to use copper mesh to make a connection to the glass cell. The glass cell was pre-scratched in the area where the mesh and wires were supposed to go. But . . . even with the copper mesh, it didn't stick. It was doable, but difficult, and not very strong. All the wires pulled off. Some of you may have had success with using copper mesh soldered to scratched areas of glass cells, but there is an easier way. Perhaps you have a broken/damaged glass cell. You may still be able to use it, unless the damage has made the glass transparent, in which case there is severe damage to the photovoltaic part of the cell. One interesting thing about the glass cells: Looking at them, you see lines, just as you may on broken or crystalline cells, but those lines are not current-collecting conductors. They are gaps between areas of the glass cell that each make about half a volt. So, glass cells can be expected to have two lines for every volt of output. And they can make 6 or 9 or 12 or 20 volts. So, we want to connect the wires to places with the most amount of lines between them to get the highest voltage. And out of the wires on the silver side, of course. Scratch the silver (probably aluminum) near the edges and test the voltage and polarity. I usually use a red wire for positive and a black or green for negative. Easy connection method: You need two brass extrusions, carefully cut with a Dremel (safety goggles!), and wires soldered on this side of the extrusions Note: The extrusion must have enough space inside it for the glass cell to fit. The extrusion is then crushed a little (before putting it on the glass) so that it will bite the glass with some pressure and make contact with the scratched edge. Slide the crushed extrusion onto the glass. If it's too crushed it won't go on, so pry it open. If it's not crushed enough it falls off, so crush it more. When it bites, and there is voltage in the light across the two extrusions, put sticky tape or just a little plastic cement over the extrusion to help it stay there. The glass cell is now ready to use. The long one shown is actually two 9-volt ones on one glass, and is the one that I put extruded contacts on because the copper mesh wouldn't stick.

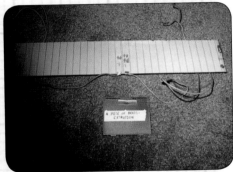

Step 5: Preparing Copper Indium Selenide Cells

These are rather well prepared already. They have easy to solder tabs and are marked which end is negative with a dash of a black marker. The ones I got, I mounted in frames and in an acrylic polymer sheet sandwich. Three in series . . . in parallel with three more in series . . . makes nice 12 volts. I have been advised that these cells undergo some kind of reaction if first exposed to full sun with no load for about 15 minutes, and that the result is good. I'm told that the result generates more output than if they are not treated this way. Just FYI. I didn't notice the difference between the panel that had pre-sunned cells and another that didn't. The cells are glass tiles that appear to be made similar to the Amorphous glass, but they are more efficient and produce around 4.5 volts and 100ma each in full sun, approximately. As they say, your mileage may vary. I have no advice for broken CIS cells. It is very easy to connect CIS cells together. Peel back the tabs a little, which point to each other under the cell, and start to peel back the sticky tape that holds it on, just enough so that you can solder them in series. And watch the polarity! I goofed it up a couple of times. No damage done, but I had to do it over. When soldering, wet the ends of the tabs with solder, then press down quickly with a popsicle stick or something to flatten them against the bottom of the cells. The cells go together nicely like tiles. With moderate carefulness, you don't need to worry much about ruining them yourself, just don't leave them alone with curious people until your panel is done and safe inside a solid frame. I've fastened them with both RTV silicone and double-sticky-foam tape. I prefer the silicone-glued result, with the cell tiles grouted against the glass from behind.

(No silicone between the cells and the frame glass.) DSFT (foam tape) is more likely to (it has, in fact) let go of a couple of the cells. As mentioned before, although I don't know if it's necessary for CIS cells, use a diode when charging batteries with the panels.

Step 6: Applications for Small Solar Panels

The solar panels I made and pictured generate around 1 or 2 watts generally. These are the applications I use them for:

- Charging batteries. In the blackout of 2003, those batteries ran our blackout party, which included black lights, fans (it was a hot day), radio, small TV, and low voltage lights. And an AC inverter. (I go to the rechargeable battery recycle bins with a meter and if they are not really dead then I borrow them until they are. I didn't buy any of these batteries.)
- Solar night lights—nowadays a very common thing where I live.
- Solar powered fans—although my solar panels run computer fans directly when it's hot (the sun makes it hot, and the sun runs the fans!), I notice that solar charged battery powered fans are *much more powerful.*
- Solar flashlights
- Solar powered radios—including my ham radio shack.

About solar-powered computers

I guess people don't leave their laptops in the sun. . . . My approach to designing a solar powered computer, (and my definition of computer is a processor with memory and a keyboard and a screen that runs not-necessarily-an-operating-system) is to use very high resistance CMOS chips, which use very little electricity, just like watches and calculators. A computer is also a calculator with lots of memory, and CMOS memory is a common thing! At nighttime, the computer has not used up all its solar power so it uses what is stored in the rechargeable battery. There is simply no demand for the solar powered computers, nor any obstacle to solar powering a PDA or a laptop with similarly sized panels.

Duty cycles

In simple theory, if you get eight hours of sun and need one hour of power, you can get by with one eighth the solar power by saving it up in batteries. Also, if LED lights should run all night, it's easy to collect more than enough solar power during the day in batteries with the right sized panel.

Step 7: Getting More Practical Power from Your Panel

It is very easy to get a few solar cells and put them together into a panel, but sometimes it gets expensive to get enough cells to make a useful voltage. If you obtained one or two large cells, you may have a whole watt or two, but only a volt or less, and that's sad. Not too many things run on less than a volt. Perhaps you got enough big broken cells to make 6 volts, but wouldn't it be nice to have 12 volts? Then maybe you could keep a battery charged and occasionally run an inverter on it. In the last step I mentioned how time could be used to save up power for another time when it will be used. And a small panel can make enough power over a long time to run a big load for a short time. In this step I am talking about matching the voltage of the panel, whatever it may be, to the voltage that you find useful. Or generally, matching supply and demand in a satisfying, practical way. It may be possible to design a 2 volt circuit for a 2 volt panel, but unnecessary. It is possible, only using germanium transistors as far as I know, to get any voltage out of a big half-volt cell, but I don't know a modern way, so I'll leave that idea alone. But there are many voltage doubler or multiplier circuits that work at slightly higher voltages, and I've made a few panels around 6 volts, which I'd like to get 12 out of. There is a voltage doubler chip still available called ICL7660 or MAX1044 that is very convenient to use. So I will use it as an example, since I'd rather have around a watt at 12 volts than at 6 volts. There is something else I did that was very obvious in the picture for step 1, where I had three broken cell panels around 6 volts and put them in series to get around 18 volts . . . and since the cells were large, that array has a lot of current. But if I use just one 6 volt panel and want 12 volts, I use the voltage doubler and get twice the voltage in exchange for half the current. AC transformers do the same thing . . . almost the same power goes out as goes in, but at a more useful voltage. Some circuits that do this are called "DC to DC converters".

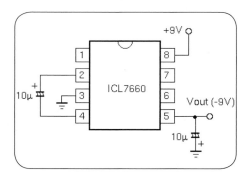

Solar Lawn Mower!

By marsh
(www.instructables.com/id/Solar-Lawn-Mower-1/)

I've had battery powered lawn mowers before and they are a real pain to keep charged. You have to either plug them in or take the battery out and that sucks.

This is one solution to the problem. Install solar panels on the mower and just leave it parked in the sun to charge it.

Here's how I did it!

Tools and Materials Needed

Tools
- soldering iron
- wire stripper
- volt meter
- screwdriver
- wrenches

Materials
- battery-powered lawnmower
- (2)12 volt photovoltaic solar panels
- 4 general purpose rectifier diodes
- double-stick tape
- nuts, bolts, and washers
- solder

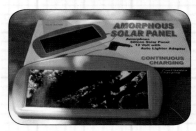

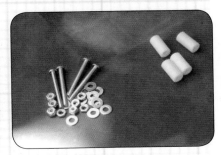

Step 1: Evaluate the Lawnmower's Current Condition

I had a DR Neuton Mower, but this Toro came up on Freecycle (www. freecycle.org). It was way more mondo than the DR, so I decided it would be the donor machine.

The first thing I did was check the batteries. They were toast, so I had to build a new battery pack.

I got four replacement batteries at my local electronic supply for $18.00 each. To keep them as a cohesive pack, I applied double-stick tape between each battery, just like the original setup had.

Step 2: How to Wire It Up

A photovoltaic (PV) solar cell has a power output recognized in watts. When the sun is shining, the potential of the PV cell is greater than that of the batteries, so energy will flow from the PV cells to the batteries.

But what happens when the sun goes down? Then the batteries have a greater potential. That means that if you don't take steps to prevent it, energy will flow

285

from the batteries to the PV cells. This energy will be wasted as heat emanated from the PV cells, ultimately burning them out and draining the batteries.

We can prevent this by installing diodes in the circuit. A diode is like a one-way check valve for electricity. It makes it possible for the solar panel to charge the battery, but impossible for the battery to heat the solar panel.

The circuit below shows the typical wiring for this type of application. This system uses four 6 volt batteries and is charged by two 12 volt solar panels. The overall system voltage is 24 volts. When you line up batteries, their voltage adds as you place more in the series. The panels are 12 volts so we need to isolate them from each other. The diodes also accomplish this task.

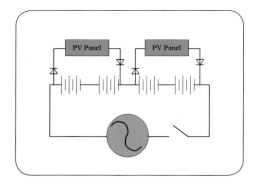

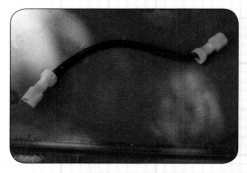

Step 3: Hook up the Batteries

Returning to the battery pack. Let's treat these four batteries as two sets of two. Hook them together as shown and test the voltage to make sure they show 12 volts per pair. OCV (open-circuit voltage) may be on the order of 14 volts. This is normal. In fact, if it's below 10 volts you may have a bad battery. Finally, there will be an interconnect between the two sets. As shown in the schematic, we need to tap this interconnect to hook up our PV cells. Do this using a wire stripper. Do not cut the wire, just breach and separate the insulation.

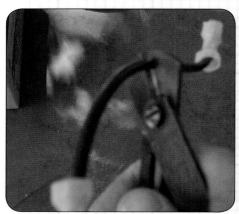

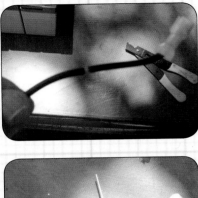

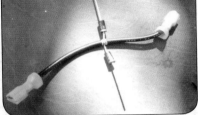

Step 4: Install the Power Taps

Just as we did on the interconnect, breach the positive power lead and install a diode. Make sure the band on the diode is closest to the red wire.

Step 5: Repeat the Process

Do the same thing again on the negative side.

This time make sure the band of the diode is facing away from the black wire.

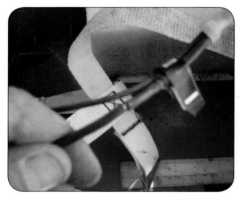

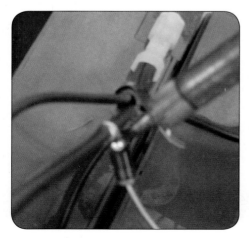

Step 6: Scavenge Some Parts

With this PV panel came a cigar lighter plug. Yes, I said cigar lighter. Read your owner's manual. That heat source is a CIGAR lighter.

We're not going to use it, but we need to take a look at it.

First, cut the PV connector off. Leave a foot or so of wire on it and strip the ends.

Set that aside and let's look at what we have left.

Open up the cigar lighter plug. There's a circuit board in there. What do you think it does?

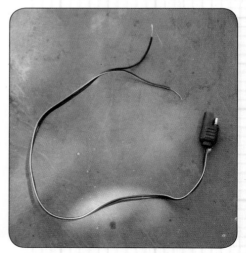

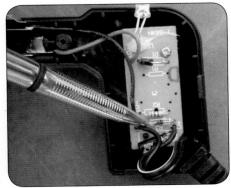

Step 7: Continuing with the Wiring

We're now ready to connect the power taps to the PV power plugs.

Slide heat shrink tubing over the wire *before* soldering the wire to the diode. Attach the wires to the diodes and solder them in place. Next, slide the shrink tubing over the solder joint and the diode and shrink it down to insulate the joint.

289

Make sure to get the polarity right! The stripped wire from the PV panel is positive. Make sure this wire is connected to a diode that points toward a positive terminal of the battery. I've tried to make it clear on how to make this determination.

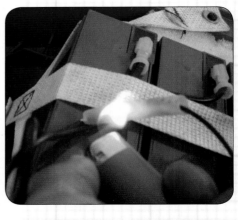

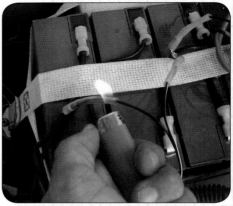

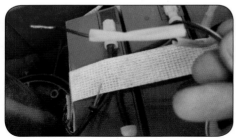

Step 8: Check Your Wiring!

At this point you should have two connectors wired through diodes to the batteries. Check these with a volt meter; there should be no voltage present. The diodes are a one-way check valve for electricity from the PV panels to the batteries, not the reverse.

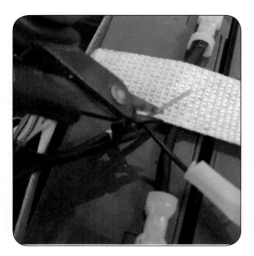

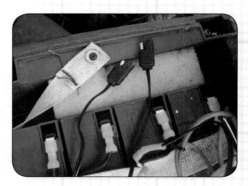

holes for the PV panels. Next, cut spacers to conform to the contour of the motor cover. Don't forget, it's all plastic and the stuff flexes really well. It's pretty forgiving.

In this installation there were some reinforcements on the underside that had to be removed. Tin snips and an X-ACTO knife took care of the offending plastic pretty quickly.

Use the other half of the contour-cut spacer to shim the bottom of the mounting.

Step 9: Continue Checking Your Wiring

At this point you're all wired up and you can make some voltage checks to make sure you can safely proceed.

Step 10: Mount the PV Panels

Now that the hard part is out of the way, let's get to the easy stuff.

These panels have keyhole shaped mounting holes. Place a screw in the hole and tighten a nut down over it. This gives you a stud mounting. Align the stud onto the cover and drill mounting

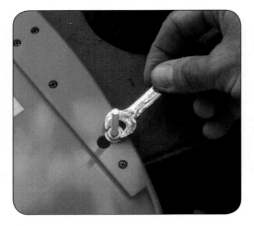

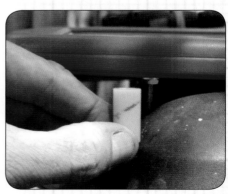

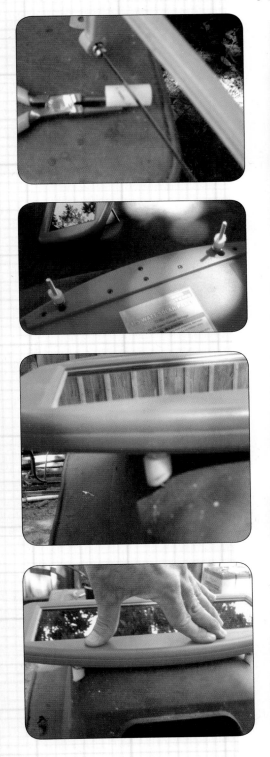

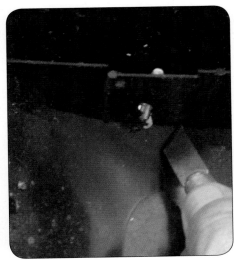

Step 11: Run the Wiring

Now that the PV panels are mounted, run the wires into the motor cover.

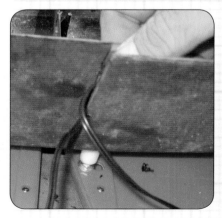

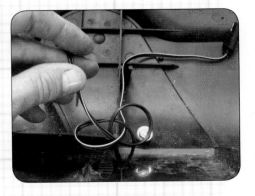

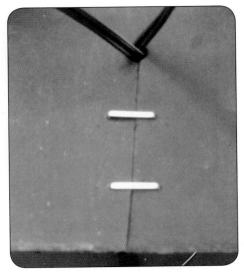

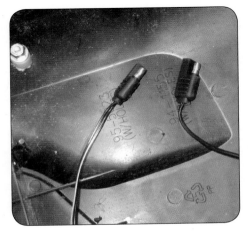

Step 12: Check the Solar Panel Output

OCV (open-circuit voltage) of these PV panels is on the order of 16 to 20 volts. If it is especially light out, this is the reading you should get.

Step 14: There It Is!

It works and really works well. I've been mowing my lawn every day for three days and the mower is fully charged every time I turn it on. All I need now is a lawn.

Step 13: The Final Hookup!

Connect the PV panels to the battery banks.

Next, check your voltages. You should have two banks of 12 to 15 volts and the overall voltage should be at least 24 volts.

Solar-Powered Fountain/Herb Garden

By James Harrigan
(sleighbedguy)
(www.instructables.com/id/Solar-powered-fountainherb-garden/)

- 4" ABS pipe (2' segment)
- 4" end caps
- (2) 3/8" vinyl tubing
- shrink tubing
- wire
- epoxy
- ABS pipe cement
  Tools
- drill
- saw (handsaw, band saw, jigsaw, or miter saw)
- router (useful)
- lathe (optional)

Here is a simple garden fountain utilizing a $20 solar panel/pump combo, some sewer pipe, bamboo, and a strawberry pot. The fountain will only run in direct sunlight, but the herbs will thrive in the same conditions. This one isn't hard to do, and again doesn't require any special tools. Everything should run you about $50.

Gather the Materials

- floating solar fountain (from Harbor Freight Tools)
- bamboo
- clear spray lacquer
- strawberry pot

Step 1: Disassemble the Fountain

This is waterproof and, therefore, taking it apart is a bit of a pain. In my case, Harbor Freight sent the wrong item as a replacement and I do not have a pool . . . so this was my only option. Flip over the fountain. Along the bottom are circular bumps. Drill through each one with room to spare. If this does not loosen it, you will have to cut the two halves apart. Your reward for this arduous task will be a pump and two solar panels. This was the by far the hardest step!

Step 2: Cut the Pipe and Bamboo

The fountain does not need to utilize bamboo, I just *really* like it. Cut the bamboo to the height you want. The fountain is supposed to have 19.5 inches of lift. Remember the water is traveling from the bottom of the pot. Measure the pipe with one cap on. After the two halves are dry-fitted, it should fit like it does in the picture below. I used a band saw, so I haven't provided a measurement. The pot might be different, and we all know no one can just draw a straight line around a cylinder. This might be a bit of trial and error. The bamboo I chose to use has the nifty little spout. This was cut on the band saw, then the horrible cut was covered with twine (epoxied in place) to hide the flaws. The sewer caps are $6 a piece, and I glued the top on first. I chose to save the $6 and make the project harder. The caps

are also domed, so I routed a small trough near the edge and drilled some drainage holes to capture most of the water. Due to another one of my mistakes, I had to make the plug to hold the bamboo upright. This isn't necessary. If you don't have a lathe, the large hole will need to fit the end of your bamboo. Or you can epoxy the bamboo to the cap. Just remember to drill for the wire and the tubing. I left out the wiring/solar panel portion. There are only two wires. Be sure to use the shrink tubing to make sure the wires are fairly well protected from the water.

Step 3: Dry Fitting

Assemble the fountain without gluing anything in place. If you use the a plug to hold the bamboo upright as I did, make sure the wire and tubing clear the cap and that the wire can get out of the pot. Another issue I found with my original configuration was that the spout was too long. I had to cut it nearly in half. It is better to find this out before it is totally assembled! If everything fits, lacquer up the bamboo and twine. When it's dry, you're all set.

around the edges of the pipe to keep the water from draining off as quickly. It has been two days, and the water is getting to the plants, but keeping the fountain running. For the solar panels, I chose to use the part of the fountain already containing everything just because it was easier than building another setup. If you do plan to make your own container for the solar panels, use super glue and clear acrylic. I did some tests with this, and it works very well.

Step 4: Plant Those Herbs and Enjoy

Some contrasting rocks hide the ABS pipe and really cap off the whole fountain. I had to add some clear vinyl

Greenhouse from Old Windows

By Michael Taeuber (cheft)
(www.instructables.com/
id/Greenhouse-From-Old-
Windows/)

almost 10 percent of what a greenhouse kit would cost. The size I built was 7 feet high × 10 feet deep × 6 feet wide. But the size of your greenhouse will depend on your windows and the time you want to put into the project.

This is a brief guide on how I took some old windows from houses they were tearing down in my neighborhood and turned them into a small greenhouse in my backyard. I collected the windows over the course of a year and a half and the build took about three months, spending one day a week on it. I spent about $300 for the lumber for the frame and screws, caulk, latches, etc. That's

Step 1: Collect Windows and Plan Two Pair of Equal Sides

Look for old windows and save every one you get. After you have many, lay them out and play a game trying to make two pairs of "walls" both the same height. Two to three inches won't matter as you can cover the difference with wood. Smaller holes will need to have glass cut for them or filled with something else. Keep in mind that one end will need a door and the other a hole for a fan.

Step 2: Create a Frame

Using the windows you chose as a guide, construct a frame for each wall. Use good lumber for this, as it is the structure that holds all the weight. I used all 2 × 4s for the studs and 4 × 4s for the corner posts. Choose a length that allows at least 14 inches of the stud to be placed in the ground for support.

Step 3: Brace the Walls

Start placing the walls up, bracing them well so they don't fall over. Be sure to check that they are level.

Step 4: Make the Foundation Secure

To avoid certain problems with pesky city building permits, I built the structure shed height and did not pour a concrete foundation. Instead I buried cinder blocks to stabilize the 4 × 4 corner posts. They keep it from moving an inch.

Step 5: Screw on Windows

I used some nice coated deck screws to affix the windows to the frame. This will allow for easy removal and replacement if any break. This side facing the camera has the empty window for a fan.

Step 6: Get a Floor

I was able to find someone who needed rocks removed from their yard. Using rocks or stones is good for two reasons: good drainage and heat storage.

Step 7: Build the Roof

This was tricky. I ended up getting siding from an old shed someone had torn down. Any material you use, look for lightweight and waterproof material. Be sure that you have some that will open for ventilation, at least 20 to 30 percent of your floor space. You can get by with less if you use a fan for ventilation. Also build the slant roof with at least a 4-degree pitch, otherwise rain may not sheet off well.

Step 8: Add the Shelves and Fans

I found an old picnic bench and this fan and shelf in the garbage. I figured I could use them in my greenhouse and save them from a landfill.

Step 9: Caulk and Paint

Use a good outdoor caulk and seal all the cracks and holes between the windows. Paint the wood to protect it from the weather.

Step 10: Winter

One winter was especially bad near me. We had several feet of snow weeks on end. Luckily, I had already emptied the greenhouse and removed the roof panels in late November. I live in a zone five area. During the last month I brought out an electric heater to keep the temperature more consistent overnight.

Later I was able to obtain a large picture window and decided to install a windowed roof in the spring. It will allow much more light in and therefore heat. I used the same deck screws to affix the windows to the roof frame I already had built. For the roof vents, I took two windows and screwed them together. I found old door hinges and used a piece of PVC as a brace. I added a screw holding it to the frame as a cotter pin. Lastly, in case a huge gust of wind came along and tried to yank open the windows, I nailed a small chain to the frame and window to prevent the window slamming backwards onto the rest of the roof.

I also modified the south facing bench. It connects to the frame on one end and still uses cinder blocks on the other. This will hopefully allow me to utilize the space inside better. It's filling quickly!

Now that the roof will allow so much light through, cooling will be a greater issue this summer. I may place some of the old panels back up in July or August to reflect some of that light. I also obtained some reflecting fabric.

Lastly, I think in the future, I will completely rebuild the roof, using the windows for a gable type structure. It will force me to use some sort of poly material to cover up the gable ends. The current pitch of the roof is not enough to slope water off the windows completely.

Step 11: Fan Window

I was unhappy with having to remove the fan/vent window and having to prop it against something while cooling the greenhouse during the day. The frame was already designed to fit the window into it. I decided to have it slide up and be held in place. I started by salvaging some hinges from an old entertainment center. They are the kind that sit completely outside the door. Plus these had a unique shape that fit around a right angle. This allowed the wooden "stops" to swing in place and hold the window up while I was venting or when the fan is in place. Across the frame I nailed some boards to hold the fan window against the frame. Lastly, I found an old pulley and fastened it to the window so I can pull it up easily.

Step 12: Spring Roof Vent Upgrades

Had a major score! A local community greenhouse was torn down and replaced. I was able to get some great parts. Here is a picture of the new window system. It originally opened the windows on the side of the greenhouse. The wheel is turned and rotates the gear attached to the pipe, opening the windows, which makes opening and shutting easy. While every window now must be open at the same time, I can control the angle at which they are open.

Also pictured is a gutter claimed from the trash. The hinge side of the roof windows always leaked profusely. The gutter catches the water and stores it in a bucket for easy watering.

Step 14: Winter Two Years Later

Here is the greenhouse in a mild winter. I overwinter many potted perennials inside. To insulate the roof, I stretch a sheet of poly across the top to keep out the drafts. Last October, I repainted both the inside and out. All the wood is doing well. I hope that, with care, the greenhouse will last over ten years. It has changed the way I garden, making my backyard much more productive.

Step 13: Spring Shading

Bought some secondhand rolling shades that are working great. They easily roll up and down the south facing wall while not taking up too much room.

An Algae Bioreactor from Recycled Water Bottles

By Michael H. Fischer

(mfischer)

(www.instructables.com/id/An-Algae-Bioreactor-from-Recycled-Water-Bottles/)

In this Instructable, we describe how to build a photo-bioreactor that uses algae to convert carbon dioxide and sunlight into energy. The energy that is produced is in the form of algae biomass. The photo-bioreactor is built from plastic recycled water bottles. By designing the apparatus to be compartmentalized, we are able to do many experiments in parallel. By using algae as a biofuel, we can increase the world's supply of oil while at the same time we decrease the amount of atmospheric carbon dioxide used during its production. The resulting product is a sustainable biofuel whose carbon footprint is neutral inasmuch as the CO_2 produced on consumption is essentially balanced by the CO_2 used in its production. In this Instructable, we first make the carbon dioxide delivery system, then mount the water bottles on a rack, and then inoculate the bottles with algae. After letting the algae grow for a week, we extract the biomass.

Step 1: Make Carbon Dioxide Delivery System

To make the carbon dioxide delivery system, connect an eight-port sprinkler system manifold to a 1" long PVC pipe. To get good seals, use Teflon tape to tape the threads before attaching the pieces together. Next, attach the 1" pipe

to a T-connector. Block off one end of the T-connector and attach the other end to 1' long PVC pipe.

Step 2: Attach Tubing to Manifold

For each manifold, cut eight pieces of flexible tubing and connect each piece to a port of the manifold. The manifold that I am using has a dial on each port to control the rate of flow. Make sure all the ports that you use are open and allow approximately the same amount of carbon dioxide to flow through the port.

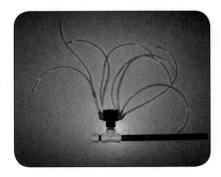

Step 3: Mount Carbon Dioxide System

Mount the air system to a metal rack using zip ties. Attach the air system to a tank of carbon dioxide.

Step 4: Mount Water Bottles

Hot glue the water bottles to the metal rack.

Step 5: Make Algae Media

We next make the medium to grow the algae. Although there are many possible mediums, a standard garden store fertilizer contains all the nitrogen and nutrients that the algae need.

Step 6: Media Inoculation

A good source of algae is pond algae, if available. If not, there are a large number of online vendors that sell batches of algae. To inoculate the culture, measure out a fixed amount of algae and add it to the growth medium.

extract the algae from the solution. The biomass of the dried algae can then be used as a fuel. As a by-product of this process, a large amount of atmospheric CO_2 is sequestered.

Step 7: Growth and Harvesting

After several days of sunlight and CO_2 exposure, the algae are much denser. A French press is then used to

CONVERSION TABLES

One person's inch is another person's centimeter. Instructables projects come from all over the world, so here's a handy reference guide that will help keep your project on track.

Measurement								
	1 Millimeter	1 Centimeter	1 Meter	1 Inch	1 Foot	1 Yard	1 Mile	1 Kilometer
Millimeter	1	10	1,000	25.4	304.8	—	—	—
Centimeter	0.1	1	100	2.54	30.48	91.44	—	—
Meter	0.001	0.01	1	0.025	0.305	0.91	—	1,000
Inch	0.04	0.39	39.37	1	12	36	—	—
Foot	0.003	0.03	3.28	0.083	1	3	—	—
Yard	—	0.0109	1.09	0.28	033	1	—	—
Mile	—	—	—	—	—	—	1	0.62
Kilometer	—	—	1,000	—	—	—	1.609	1

Volume									
	1 Milliliter	1 Liter	1 Cubic Meter	1 Teaspoon	1 Tablespoon	1 Fluid Ounce	1 Cup	1 Pint	1 Quart	1 Gallon
Milliliter	1	1,000	—	4.9	14.8	29.6	—	—	—	—
Liter	0.001	1	1,000	0.005	0.015	0.03	0.24	0.47	0.95	3.79
Cubic Meter	—	0.001	1	—	—	—	—	—	—	0.004
Teaspoon	0.2	202.9	—	1	3	6	48	—	—	—
Tablespoon	0.068	67.6	—	0.33	1	2	16	32	—	—
Fluid Ounce	0.034	33.8	—	0.167	0.5	1	8	16	32	—
Cup	0.004	4.23	—	0.02	0.0625	0.125	1	2	4	16
Pint	0.002	2.11	—	0.01	0.03	0.06	05	1	2	8
Quart	0.001	1.06	—	0.005	0.016	0.03	0.25	.05	1	4
Gallon	—	0.26	264.17	0.001	0.004	0.008	0.0625	0.125	0.25	1

conversion tables

Mass and Weight						
	1 Gram	1 Kilogram	1 Metric Ton	1 Ounce	1 Pound	1 Short Ton
Gram	1	1,000	—	28.35	—	—
Kilogram	0.001	1	1,000	0.028	0.454	—
Metric Ton	—	0.001	1	—	—	0.907
Ounce	0.035	35.27	—	1	16	—
Pound	0.002	2.2	—	0.0625	1	2,000
Short Ton	—	0.001	1.1	—	—	1

Speed		
	1 Mile per hour	1 Kilometer per hour
Miles per hour	1	0.62
Kilometers per hour	1.61	1

Temperature		
	Fahrenheit (°F)	Celsius (°C)
Fahrenheit	—	(°C x 1.8) + 32
Celsius	(°F − 32) / 1.8	—